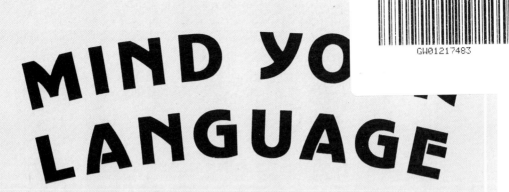

Teacher's Notes

Sue Palmer
and
Peter Brinton

Oliver & Boyd

Oliver & Boyd
Longman House
Burnt Mill
Harlow
Essex CM20 2JE

An Imprint of Longman Group UK Ltd

ISBN 0 05 004260 2
First published 1988
Third impression 1990
© Oliver & Boyd 1988

All rights reserved; no part of this
publication may be reproduced, stored in a
retrieval system, or transmitted in any form
or by any means, electronic, mechanical,
photocopying, recording or otherwise without
either the written permission of the Publishers
or a licence permitting restricted copying in the
United Kingdom issued by the Copyright Licensing
Agency Ltd, 33-34 Alfred Place, London, WC1E 7DP.

Set 10/12 pt Aster
Produced by Longman Group (FE) Ltd
Printed in Hong Kong

CONTENTS

	page
Introduction	
Children's Language	5
Spoken and Written Language	5
Language Awareness	5
The Teaching of Grammar	6
How the Series Works	6
Pupils' Books	7

Book One
   Chapter   1 — Words, Words, Words   9
                2 — Sense and Sentences   10
                3 — What is a Noun?   11
                4 — Proper Nouns: Names and Addresses   12
                5 — How do you ask a Question?   14
                6 — Verbs   15
                7 — Phrases and Sentences   16
                8 — Punctuation Marks   17
                9 — Adjectives   19

Book Two
   Chapter   1 — What is Language For?   21
                2 — Common and Proper Nouns   22
                3 — Verbs and Sentences   23
                4 — Adjectives: Making Sentences Grow   25
                5 — Parts of Speech: Pronouns   26
                6 — Sentences and Subjects   28
                7 — Punctuation: Making Sense with Sentences   30
                8 — Punctuation: Using Punctuation Marks   31
                9 — Punctuation: The Apostrophe   32
              10 — Spoken Language versus Written Language   34

Book Three
   Chapter   1 — Parts of Speech: Nouns, Verbs, Adjectives   35
                2 — Tense: Past, Present, Future   36
                3 — Nouns and Pronouns: Singular and Plural   38
                4 — Subject and Verb: Agreement   39
                5 — Parts of Speech: Adverbs   41
                6 — Punctuation Marks   43
                7 — Speaking and Writing: Clear Enough?   44
                8 — Paragraphs: Chunks of Information   46
                9 — Two-Clause Sentences   47
              10 — Find the Main Clause   49
              11 — Direct Speech   50

Book Four
- Chapter 1 — Parts of Speech — 52
- 2 — Punctuation — 54
- 3 — Capital Letters — 56
- 4 — Spoken and Written Language — 57
- 5 — Spoken and Written Language: Standard English — 58
- 6 — The Apostrophe to show Ownership — 60
- 7 — Expanding and Reducing Sentences (Subjects, Verbs and Clauses) — 61
- 8 — Subjects, Verbs and Objects — 63
- 9 — Inverted Commas — 64
- 10 — Words and Meanings: Idioms — 66
- 11 — Sorts of Sentences and Sentence Transformations — 66
- 12 — What is Language? — 68

Selected Bibliography — 70

INTRODUCTION

Children's Language

Most children, by the age of seven or eight, can use their native language, in its spoken form, quite efficiently. They can express their feelings and needs, ask questions, give simple instructions, and manipulate the spoken word in many other specialised ways. (Even those children who are unresponsive in the classroom can usually be found using language to achieve their needs in the playground!) Children are at this stage, however, largely unconscious of what they are doing. The use of language is, for them, an intuitive act, and the language they use is part and parcel of the whole situation in which they find themselves — it is, as Margaret Donaldson puts it in her book *Children's Minds* (Fontana 1978), **embedded** in the events which surround it.

If children are to develop their use of language further than this basic level, they must become more aware of it: they must learn to **disembed** it from the situations which surround it and appreciate it as an abstract system which exists independently of events and circumstances. Many educationists believe that an appreciation of language as an objective system is an important step towards reasoned thought, and that aspects of intellectual development may thus depend upon the development of linguistic awareness.

Spoken and Written Language

One important facet of linguistic awareness is an understanding that there are differences between spoken and written language. Children must come to recognise that written language is not merely "speech written down". Written language is not embedded in events, and therefore does not have the supporting *context* which accompanies a spoken message. A much greater burden of meaning therefore falls upon the written language itself, and upon the conventions by which it is set down on paper. This recognition characterises the writing of the more literate child: he/she has become aware of written language as a form in itself, and treats it differently from the language of speech.

According to some researchers, command of the written form of our language is the hallmark of what we consider the "educated mind". Without it, academic success may prove almost impossible. An understanding of how written English differs from the spoken form would seem to be, therefore, an essential part of a child's education.

Language Awareness

Awareness of language begins with an understanding of some of the common words we use to talk about the subject. "Word" and "sentence" are concepts so familiar to adults that we do not consider that many children may not be sure of their meaning. Yet research has indicated that this is often the case. And even where children can use such words in conversation, it is possible that their understanding is an implicit one — they have the general "feel" of the concepts, but not a real grasp.

They must become aware of a word as an "object", something that exists independently of its meaning, which can be talked about, written down and looked at and used in various contexts. They must also recognise that groups of words can be ordered together in particular ways to convey meaning, and that, in our language, certain other ways are not permissible.

To look further at language, children must acquire a certain amount of specialised vocabulary (what linguists call a "metalanguage"). Access to the names of the major parts of speech, of the various punctuation marks, and of some of the main elements of sentence structure, enables pupils to discuss language and to manipulate it more freely. And the more they can talk about language and discuss its use (particularly within a meaningful context), the more aware of it they will become.

The differences between spoken and written language are, of course, particularly worthwhile areas of discussion — and possession of a metalanguage allows greater and deeper understanding of these differences.

The Teaching of Grammar

The teaching of "grammar" has been the subject of much debate over the last few decades. Educational researchers have found that rote practice of grammatical points in isolation does not help to improve children's writing, and some teachers have taken this to indicate that teaching about the way language works is unnecessary. However, if we believe the arguments above, language awareness *is* important to developing literacy and abstract thought, and what used to be called "grammar" is part and parcel of this awareness. Children's linguistic education should include knowledge of the parts of speech, of sentence structure and of punctuation: all of these are elements of language of which they must become aware.

A new approach to teaching these concepts is required. If practice of grammatical points in isolation is ineffective, other methods must be employed. Overwhelmingly, recent research in education has indicated that *active processing* of information is the most effective way of learning — opportunities for discussing, investigating, and purposefully manipulating language should be provided for pupils. Pupils may then experiment with the concepts acquired through these activities in real situations — in their own written work.

We attempt in *Mind Your Language* to provide material which will involve children in *thinking* about language (often trying to work out a particular grammatical rule themselves), *discussing* its use, and *playing with* language or *manipulating* language rules to help internalise the concepts. We cover the main parts of speech, the most common punctuation marks, and the major elements of a sentence; and we combine this with work which will alert pupils to the most significant differences between spoken and written language, and thus help them to achieve increasing control over written language for themselves.

How the Series Works

The series combines contemporary ideas on learning and literacy with recent findings in linguistics, psycholinguistics and sociolinguistics. It has been extensively tested in the classroom, to ensure that the activities suggested are both practicable and successful, and the text has been subjected to considerable revision as a result of children's and teachers' comments. Both authors have taught for many years in primary schools, and have tried to ensure that the activities provided will appeal to children.

Each chapter takes a particular language point and provides discussion material through which the particular concept may be introduced. (Substantial teachers'

INTRODUCTION

notes, giving theoretical background and practical suggestions for work on the chapter, are available in this teachers' book to ensure that the teacher feels adequately informed to lead pupils' discussion.) Each chapter also includes one or more activities — games, drama, art-work, further language work — through which the concept can be developed. Finally (in response to teachers' requests) there are a number of exercises, progressing in level of difficulty, which provide practice of the language point.

These exercises will provide a written record of the areas covered and will keep the majority of a class or group usefully occupied while the teacher devotes time to specific pupils. They are included for these reasons alone, since the efficacy of exercises in developing children's language skills is highly questionable.

What *is* important is that teachers should build on what was been learned through each chapter in subsequent *purposeful* written work. Once an aspect of punctuation or part of speech has been introduced, teachers should seize opportunities to alert children to its use in everyday written English — in their creative and personal writing, in project work, in writing in History, Geography, Science, Mathematics, and so on. They should attempt to use the newly-learnt metalinguistic terms when talking about reading too, helping children to make sense of what they read. *Using language knowledge in real situations* will help to consolidate the concepts introduced in this book, and to that end is of infinitely more worth than the completion of exercises.

The four books of the series gradually build up pupils' knowledge about language. It is therefore advisable, if possible, to work through them sequentially.

Teachers' Notes

The notes on each chapter should be read through completely, alongside the chapter, before the chapter is used with a class. They provide background information, hints on organisation, suggestions for follow-up in the children's own written work and answers to the exercises at the end of the chapter. They also list, for each chapter, the linguistic vocabulary revised and introduced there.

Pupils' Books

The text of the books is addressed to the children, but is designed to be read by the class or group along with their teacher. The teacher may prefer to read the text aloud him/herself, or to assign children to read it out. Questions are asked frequently, and it is intended that these should lead into further discussion where necessary with particular groups — the teacher will be the best judge of whether a point needs further discussion or not, and can direct it appropriately.

We recommend very strongly that discussion should be as open-ended as possible, that it should be fairly light-hearted, and that children should be allowed to experiment with ideas about language without fear of being labelled "wrong" too resoundingly. While we hope that they will eventually reach the accepted "correct" answer, the opportunity to explore through discussion is just as important as arriving there. And all too often an immediately "correct" response is merely a lucky guess or a response parroted from another source — thought and discussion are, of course, much more useful than either of these.

Many of the games and activities suggested to follow up the discussion sessions can be played more than once, and indeed may be more enjoyable after a couple of practice runs. These provide an opportunity to use metalinguistic terms in a

INTRODUCTION

context, and teachers are urged to introduce the appropriate vocabulary as often as possible to help familiarise children with it.

We stress again that the exercises at the end of each chapter should not be seen as a particularly important part of the course. They do, however, provide a written record in each child's book of the language points covered, give children a little (albeit decontextualised) practice of these points and alert teachers to any need to supplement the programme. They will also help to occupy part of a class while the teacher attends to specific pupils. The teachers we consulted felt that exercises of this kind are helpful for these reasons. Exercises alone, however, will probably do nothing to increase children's language awareness. *Mind Your Language* must be seen as an integral part of the entire language curriculum — a means of alerting children to facets of language which they can explore thoroughly through their own purposeful language work.

BOOK ONE

CHAPTER 1
Words, Words, Words

The main purpose of this chapter is to introduce children to the study of language by alerting them to the idea of words as "objects of study".

Young children initially react to words entirely in terms of their *meaning*, and even by the age of 7+ some children may still find it difficult to look at words in an objective way. They may, indeed, not even be sure what a "word" is.

The unit looks at words in three ways:
1) length (this also gives an opportunity to check that children know the meaning of "letter");
2) arbitrariness of meaning (one word with two or more disparate meanings);
3) emotive or onomatopaeic qualities (where meaning *is* bound up in some way with the word).

Teachers should use the material on pages 4 and 5 as starting points for discussion, with the aim of encouraging children to treat words as *objects*, which can be talked about, played with, etc.

Children who are linguistically aware will be quick to respond to these ideas, as many of them will have recognised these attributes of words for themselves and experimented with them in their play activities. Such children should be able to complete the exercises at the end of the chapter more-or-less unaided (after reading them through with the teacher).

Children who are less linguistically aware may need more directed help — perhaps looking again at some of the examples in the chapter, or similar examples made up by the teacher, while the more able children are working on the exercises.

A word is generally an arbitrary thing which (excepting onomatopaeic words) has no connection with its meaning (e.g. there is no reason, beyond historical ones, why a door should be called a "door" as opposed to a "blip" or a "hippopotamus"). Hearing words from other languages and noting the differences between them and their English counterparts can help children to realise this. Many schools now include bilingual pupils, who can be a very valuable resource in this respect. We suggest at the end of the chapter that bilingual pupils might offer examples of words in other languages. Individual teachers might find ways of exploiting this resource further, both in this chapter and the following ones.

Answers to Exercises *pages 8–9 pupil's book*

Words

A Language is made up of *words*. When we talk we put words together to make *sense* (*sentences* also acceptable here). All words have *meanings*. Some words have more than one *meaning*.

B 1) penny — a small coin
2) easy — not difficult

3) ear — the part of the body you hear with
4) ankle — it joins your foot to your leg
5) lemon — a fruit with a sour taste
6) rattle — a baby's toy
7) yellow — a colour
8) aeroplane — a flying machine

C 1) Any three words with less than three letters.
2) Any three words with more than nine letters.
3) Any short word with a big meaning.
4) Any long word with a little meaning.

D Pictures and labels for two meanings for each word:
1) ring 2) match 3) stamp 4) glasses 5) letter 6) fan.

E Correctly labelled pictures of:
1) leek, leak 2) flower, flour 3) hare, hair 4) sea, see.

> **Vocabulary**
> *Introduces:* word, meaning.

CHAPTER 2
Sense and Sentences

"The sentence" is an important concept in any language course. Before children can be expected to write in sentences, punctuating them correctly, they must have some idea of what a sentence is. It is introduced here as "a group of words that make sense", and the basic punctuation (full stop/capital letter) is described. Those children who progress to the written exercises will be required to use these conventions of punctuation, but they are not at present our first concern. More important is that children acquire the concept of "sentence".

The first exercise requires children to *recognise* sentences. Most children of 7+ can do this easily with a little practice. It is suggested that the teacher makes up further examples of the type given in the chapter as necessary.

Next, the expansion of "baby-talk" into explicit, meaningful sentences gives children the opportunity to generate sentences for themselves. The baby-talk examples provide content-words embedded in a context (a picture) and dependent on that context for their interpretation. In expanding these into sentences children should make them more explicit, and context-independent. The teacher should allow a number of children to attempt the task each time and let the class judge the most successful. The teacher's task is to guide the children towards an appreciation of what makes a successful sentence.

The "Baby-Talk Play" gives all children an opportunity to practise this sentence-expansion activity.

After the various baby-talk activities, we have offered a few discussion questions to help children look objectively at what they have been doing with language. Probably only the most linguistically-aware children will be able to make much headway with these. The teacher can adjust, expand or add to these questions in the light of the class' ability and success (or otherwise!) with the chapter.

BOOK ONE

Answers to Exercises *pages 15–17 pupil's book*

Sentences

A A group of words that go together to make sense is called a *sentence*. In writing, we always start a sentence with a *capital letter*. Here are the capital letters:

A B C D E F G H I J K L M N O P Q R S T U V W X Y Z.

In writing, we end a sentence with a *full stop*.
Here are some full stops...........

B 1) A sentence makes sense.
2) It starts with a capital letter.
3) It ends with a full stop.

C

Sentences	Not Sentences
The cat went to sleep.	four hundred and six
The sky is blue.	the blue sky
Children go to school.	dog big is

D Expansions into proper sentences of:
1) want sleep
2) no play ball
3) mummy shops
4) fat cat milk

E See text book for pictures: each requires baby-talk version and proper sentence-expansion.

> **Vocabulary**
> *Revises:* word, meaning.
> *Introduces:* sentence, full stop, capital letter.

CHAPTER 3
What is a Noun?

The noun is the first part of speech to be introduced as it is, perhaps, the easiest to conceptualise. The course includes teaching about parts of speech for two reasons:
1) categorisation of words according to their function aids objective study of language;
2) the ability to talk *about* words, using technical vocabulary, is of use in analysing language generally.

This chapter, then, begins the development of the pupils' technical linguistic vocabulary, so that they can talk *about* language.

Research indicates that children acquire language by their own active mental processing of the linguistic data to which they are exposed in everyday life. They hear adults talking, and they gradually puzzle out how to use language themselves. We have tried with the Nodrog story to create a "language-puzzle" of the type which children encounter regularly in language, and through which they achieve increasing clarification of linguistic concepts.

Some children in the class may see immediately that all the words are "naming words", although they may not be able to put this understanding into words.

BOOK ONE

Others may not see it at all. However, a chance to tussle with the problem should be of more use to all children than a simple statement by the teacher that "a noun is a naming word". Teachers are therefore urged to persevere with the "Nodrog game", to allow as many children as possible to puzzle out the meaning of "noun" for themselves. All that is required at this stage is that they *produce* nouns and *recognise* nouns. They do not need to work out a definition for themselves.

The "Alphabetical Nouns" game can be played a number of times over the days following the children's work on the chapter, to reinforce the concept of nouns. Once children are able to do it fairly easily, the introduction of a memory-element can generate further interest. Each player has to repeat the entire list of nouns so far — so that the child doing *F*, for instance, could end up saying "Andrew, Betty, Catherine, Derek, Eric, *Fred*." Even further interest can be generated if the teacher promises to do Z!

Answers to Exercises *pages 26–27 pupil's book*

Nouns

A A *noun* is a naming word. It can be the name of a *person*, a *place* or a *thing*.

B 1) Any three names of people — do not penalise if capital letter is missing.
2) Any three names of places — again, do not penalise for missed capital letters.
3) Any three names of things.

C 1) Nodrog was from Sammi.
2) Nodrog landed in the playground in his spaceship.
3) Miss Wilkins was the teacher.
4) Nodrog went to the staffroom for a cup of coffee.

D Suitable nouns should have been filled into the spaces in these sentences:
1) The ...... was wearing a blue ....
2) I like to eat ....
3) The ...... went to ...... for a holiday.
4) A ...... ran into the classroom.

E Four sentences should have been composed, containing the nouns given:
1) cat, bird, tree.
2) Jane, computer, birthday.
3) teacher, children, sums.
4) spacemen, rocket, Mars.

> **Vocabulary**
> *Revises:* sentence, capital letter, full-stop.
> *Introduces:* noun.

CHAPTER 4
Proper Nouns: Names and Addresses

This chapter first provides an opportunity for revision of the concept of "nouns". *Proper nouns* are introduced as a "special sort of noun" and limited here to names and addresses, which are the types of proper nouns children should find most easy to identify. However, any proper nouns occurring in children's reading henceforth can be pointed out to those pupils who might be expected to benefit from extension of the concept.

We take the opportunity in this chapter to teach the meaning of "forename" and "surname" and to introduce simple formfilling.

The main aim of the chapter is to teach a punctuation rule: that proper nouns are written with an initial capital letter. Discussion of the meaning of forenames and the invention of names and addresses of "Silly Animals" provide opportunities for the illustration and practice of this rule.

NB. Occasionally, children may over-generalise from this chapter and start writing all nouns with initial capital letters. The teacher can have a word with such children individually to put the matter straight. It's not worth mentioning it to the whole class, as bringing the topic up might confuse some children who otherwise would not dream of over-generalising.

Answers to Exercises *pages 34–35 pupil's book*

Proper Nouns

A Special names for people and places are called *proper nouns*. We begin them with a *capital letter*. Your first name is called your *forename* and your last name is called your *surname*.

B
```
              Form About Me

   Forename(s):
   Surname:              Filled in for each individual.
   Address:
   I have ____ brother(s) and ____ sister(s).
   Their forename(s) are:
```

C 1) Child should have written his/her own name and address, set out correctly (as on an envelope).
2) Child should have written names and addresses of at least two friends, again set out correctly.

D 1) The children's names were Susan, Paul and Lucy.
2) The name Roger comes from Germany.
3) The name Ben comes from Greece.
4) There are three countries in Britain — England, Scotland and Wales.
5) There is an island called Ireland off the coast of Britain.

> **Vocabulary**
> *Revises:* noun, capital letter.
> *Introduces:* proper noun, forename, surname.

BOOK ONE

CHAPTER 5
How do you ask a Question?

This chapter has two main aims:
1) to ensure pupils' understanding of the concept of a "question", and to alert them to the characteristics of questions in spoken language.
(Although children of 7+ are quite capable of asking questions, their understanding of the form is often implicit, and they need help to see the differences between questions and statements.)
2) to introduce the question mark as a means of marking questions in written language.

Awareness of the differences between spoken and written language is extremely important in the development of literacy. The question-sentence is a good medium for introducing discussion of these differences, as tone/expression in spoken language must be represented by a punctuation mark in the written version.

NB. Teachers should ensure that children do not mistakenly conceptualise "questions" as different from "sentences". Questions should be seen as a particular type of sentence — a subset of the set of sentences. The question mark is therefore a "specialised full stop".

Answers to Exercises *page 39 pupil's book*

Questions

A In writing, we show we are asking a question by putting a *question mark* at the end of the sentence.

B Any *three* of the following:
Why can't two elephants go swimming at the same time?
Because they've only got one pair of trunks between them.

Why did the skeleton not go to the ball?
Because he had no body to go with.

Knock knock. Who's there? Ivor. Ivor who?
Ivor sore hand from knocking on your door.

Knock knock. Who's there? Mister. Mister Who?
Mister last bus home.

Knock knock. Who's there? Lemmy. Lemmy who?
Lemmy in and I'll tell you.

C Pupil should have written a list of "questioning words", e.g.:
How? What? Where? When? Which? Why? Who?

D In this exercise, any question which would be answerable by the sentences in the book is acceptable but these are the most likely:

1) How old are you?
2) Where were you born?
3) What is your name?
4) What is the teacher's name?

5) Where do kangaroos live?
6) How far is the sun from the earth?

> **Vocabulary**
> *Revises:* sentence.
> *Introduces:* question, question mark.

CHAPTER 6
Verbs

(Nouns are briefly revised at the beginning of this chapter, to reintroduce the idea of words being categorised by their function in a sentence. We have given a minimum of revision material for this in the chapter, but individual teachers can expand it as necessary before proceeding to discuss verbs. They may wish, for instance, to play the game "Alphabetical Nouns" once or twice, to ensure that pupils have remembered what a noun is.)

Again, we have tried to present pupils with an opportunity to extrapolate the function of a part of speech from samples of language. It is recommended that the teacher reads the three samples aloud while the pupils follow in their books (or appoints able readers to read the passage aloud), and then gives the pupils a few minutes to look at the underlined words and consider what they have in common. If suitable answers are not forthcoming, children could be asked to read aloud just the underlined words in the recipe and think again.

Even if no pupil is able to give a suitable explanation of verbs, many children may still be able to continue successfully with the chapter — understanding of linguistic features is often implicit, and children can often recognise and deal with ideas without being able to define them.

If nobody has satisfactorily explained what verbs are by the end of the chapter, the teacher can offer the definition that verbs are *doing* words.

The games given in the chapter can be played repeatedly whenever there are odd minutes available, to reinforce the concept.

Answers to Exercises *pages 45–46 pupil's book*

Verbs

A Verbs are *doing* words. Sometimes two or three words are grouped together to make a *verb group*.

B 1) any ten verbs.
2) any three verb groups.

C 1) I eat ice-cream.
2) The policeman rushed into the room.
3) A space ship landed in the playground.

D 1) I was eating ice-cream.
2) The policeman will rush into the room.
3) A space ship has landed in the playground.

E 1) The man <u>was driving</u> a red car.
    2) The dog <u>jumped</u> over a fence.
    3) I <u>like</u> baked beans.

F Sentences containing the following words, with verbs and verb groups underlined:
    1) baby, rattle, cot.
    2) lion, cage, zoo.
    3) witch, spell, wand.
    4) ghost, chains, house.
    5) driver, car, motorway.

> **Vocabulary**
> *Revises:* nouns.
> *Introduces:* verb, verb group.

CHAPTER 7
Phrases and Sentences

This chapter has a four-fold purpose:
1) to revise the idea of "a verb", which was introduced in the preceding chapter;
2) to revise the concept of "a sentence", introduced in Chapter 2;
3) to provide an early opportunity for the use of technical linguistic vocabulary in defining a task ("Find the *verbs* in the following *sentences*");
4) to give guidance and practice in the forming of complete sentences in response to questions. Some children find it easy to adapt part of a question to create a complete sentence in a written response. Others, however, will benefit from demonstration and discussion of the technique. Skill in answering questions in complete sentences will be of use in many areas of the curriculum.

The unit begins with a review of the concept of sentences. The teacher should expand the practice as necessary for his/her class. Another feature of sentences is then introduced: the presence of a verb. We have not devoted space here to revision of the concept of "the verb", and have merely required that the children identify verbs in context. If, however, the teacher considers it necessary to revise the meaning of "verb", he/she can use one of the games given in the preceding chapter.

The illustration of *spoken* phrases in response to *spoken* questions uses the technique of speech bubbles. The teacher may wish to help clarify this by employing pupils as "actors" to speak the words.

The illustration of *written* sentences in response to *written* questions depicts "text book questions" and "exercise book answers". It may be worth discussing the sort of occasions on which children are required to "answer in a complete sentence".

When children have expanded phrases into sentences they are asked two questions: "What are the verbs in your new sentences?" and "How did you choose which extra words to add?" The teacher may have to help in identification of the verb when it is part of the verb "to be". He/she should also ensure that all children understand that the "extra words" are gleaned from the question.

The "Answer in a Sentence Game" should provide an opportunity for children who are still unsure of the technique of creating sentence-responses to observe a number of models of the process. The teacher should choose a few able children to be IT initially, so that the less able children might benefit from observing their successful sentence-building.

Answers to Exercises *pages 51–52 pupil's book*

Phrases and Sentences

A Every sentence must have a *verb*. A group of words that does not have a *verb* is called a *phrase*. We use a lot of *phrases* when we talk, but we should always write in *sentences*.

B *Sentences*
1) The monkey <u>climbed</u> the tree.
2) I <u>like</u> school holidays.
3) James <u>ran</u> home.
4) The Queen <u>visited</u> Canada.

C *Phrases*
1) Once upon a time.
2) A black and white dog.
3) In a minute.
4) Up the street.

D Complete sentences, beginning with the following:
1) The ugly old witch......
2) A police car......
3) A little black cat......
4) Three boys......
5) The space rocket......

E Answers, in sentences, to the following questions:
1) What is your name?
2) How old are you?
3) Where do you live?
4) What is your teacher's name?
5) What is your favourite colour?
6) What do you want to be when you grow up?

> **Vocabulary**
> *Revises:* verb, sentence.
> *Introduces:* phrase.

CHAPTER 8
Punctuation Marks

Children have already met the full stop and the question mark. The generic term "punctuation marks" is now provided to describe them, and another "specialised full stop" is introduced — the exclamation mark. We have explained this as a punctuation mark which shows a "raised voice", ignoring, for the time being, other functions such as the indication of irony or humour. This simplification was con-

BOOK ONE

sidered necessary so as not to overload pupils with new information — the other functions of the exclamation mark are introduced in Book Two. (If, however, able pupils point out that other uses of the exclamation mark exist, the teacher should, of course, discuss and clarify this.)

Some teachers may object that the whole approach to punctuation in this chapter is simplistic in linguistic terms: the importance of punctuation for the "chunking" of language (dividing it into distinct units of meaning) is not yet introduced — in our examples we deal only with the punctuation of discrete sentences, not with the punctuation of complete passages of written text. This simplification is again intentional. Many children are, at 7+, unable to cope with punctuating complete passages, since their concept of the sentence is still shaky. The chapter concentrates on pressing home the importance of punctuation in writing to represent the use of the voice (and face) in speech, and pointing out the different effects gained by using different punctuation marks. The use of punctuation for breaking up passages into sentence-sized chunks is introduced in Book Two. Again, however, teachers should be prepared to discuss this aspect of the subject with individual pupils whose written work has begun to show an intuitive grasp of the concept.

We would suggest that intonation patterns in the reading of examples should be exaggerated to help children recognise different types of sentences. The picture story with speech bubbles may be best presented by three child-actors, who should stress intonation and facial expression.

The sentences on page 56 could *all* be completed by question marks if one so wished, although full stops or exclamation marks are more appropriate in some cases. Discussion with the class should establish the most suitable punctuation.

Taking Punctuation Game

Children usually need to practise the oral equivalents of the punctuation marks before they can play this game satisfactorily. If the teacher draws $\boxed{.\,!\,?}$ on the blackboard, and points to each one several times to elicit a correct and quick response, the children's oral reaction will become speedy enough to make the game enjoyable. The readers of the play script should be encouraged to pause slightly at the end of each sentence, until the "punctuation mark" has been produced by the rest of the class.

Ignore all the commas!

Answers to Exercises *pages 57–59 pupil's book*

Punctuation Marks

A We use *punctuation marks* to help make it clear what we mean in writing. A *question mark* shows the end of a *question*. A *full stop* shows the end of an ordinary *sentence*. An *exclamation mark* shows that someone is raising his voice.

B 1) A full stop looks like this — $\boxed{.}$
    2) A question mark looks like this — $\boxed{?}$
    3) An exclamation mark looks like this — $\boxed{!}$

C 1) A full stop.
    2) A question mark.
    3) An exclamation mark.

D 1) How old are you?
2) The cat is asleep by the fire.
3) Look out!
4) The biggest mountain in Britain is Ben Nevis.
5) Why do hedgehogs sleep in the winter?

E 1) Where does Karen Smith live?
2) Help!
3) Who lives in Buckingham Palace?
4) Matthew and Sam are playing in the garden.
5) Stop that noise at once!
6) Look out!
7) Is it far from here to London?
8) London is the capital of England.

F Sentences to go into speech bubbles, correctly punctuated, to accompany the following illustrations:
1) A child witnessing a bank robbery.
2) A teacher questioning a small girl about a broken window.
3) A policewoman comforting a sobbing child.
4) A father berating his child, who is watching TV.

Vocabulary
Revises: full stop, question mark, sentence.
Introduces: punctuation mark, exclamation mark.

CHAPTER 9
Adjectives

This chapter introduces a third part of speech — the adjective — in the way that nouns and verbs have already been introduced: it invites pupils to infer the function of adjectives by directed discussion of a text.

The chapter begins with revision of nouns and verbs. As before, this revision is brief: teachers should expand it, using the activities given in preceding chapters, as necessary for their classes.

As usual, pupils should be given time to puzzle out what an adjective is. Most children of 7+ will be able to identify adjectives after a little practice, but they may have difficulty defining what it is that the adjectives have in common. We provide the Glugs picture story and a number of jokes as working data.

In this chapter, however, we do eventually give a definition — "an adjective describes a noun". This is necessary to allow further work on adjectives in context.

Do not assume that children will henceforth *know* what an adjective is — being provided with a definition is no substitute for genuine conceptualisation, and further activities will be necessary for the majority of children of this age to acquire the concept.

BOOK ONE

Adjective Superhero Game
Some possible nouns for the game are:

> a baby   a teacher   a witch   a cat
> an apple   a flower   My Little Pony   Transformers

Answers to Exercises *page 64 pupil's book*

Adjectives

A *Adjectives* are words that tell you more about a *noun*. They are describing words. An *adjective* describes a *noun*.

B thin, fat, tall, short, ugly, beautiful, happy, sad, kind, mean.

C 1) The <u>little brown</u> dog licked his master.
2) Most of the time Julie wears <u>dirty old</u> jeans.
3) The monster was <u>huge</u>, <u>black</u> and <u>hairy</u>.
4) It had <u>red</u> eyes and <u>long green</u> claws.

D 1) Name of food child hates most.
2) Three adjectives to describe above.
3) Name of food child likes most.
4) Three adjectives to describe above.

E Ringing of nouns in answers to question C:
1) dog
2) jeans
3) monster
4) eyes, claws.

F Filling suitable adjectives into the spaces:
1) The .... man limped down the road.
2) The ...... lion chased the ...... deer.
3) The soup was ...... and ....
4) The ...... fireman went into the ...... house.

> **Vocabulary**
> *Revises:* noun, verb.
> *Introduces:* adjective, describes.

BOOK TWO

CHAPTER 1
What is Language For?

Two important factors in the acquisition of literacy are:
1) an appreciation of the major differences between spoken and written language;
2) an ability to look at language objectively as a symbolic system of communication.

This introductory chapter provides opportunities for the development of both these factors, through activity and discussion.

Children are required throughout the activities to think of language as a "thing", a "system" which can be looked at objectively and talked about (not merely *used* for communication). They are asked first of all to consider the functions and importance of spoken language; then they are asked to consider the same aspects of written language. Teachers may prefer to tackle the two sections on separate occasions, to help stress the difference between the spoken and written forms.

The chapter begins with an exercise which points out some of the main functions of spoken language: five examples of everyday speech are provided for matching with five categories which describe speech functions. Another four examples of speech are then given, two of which fit into categories already provided (to question, to entertain); the other two require the provision by pupils of further functional categories (giving instructions, giving orders).

Children of 8+ may find the process of categorisation by function quite difficult. It is left to the teacher whether further practice of this is worthwhile with a particular class or group. If he/she decides to pursue the question further, a video cassette of a film or T.V. serial (e.g. Grange Hill) can be useful. The teacher selects a section of the tape where speech is used for a number of different purposes. He/she then shows the section of tape right through so that pupils can appreciate the sense, and then in sections, stopping after each speech act for discussion of how language is being used in that case.

After the activity "Working Without Language", it is suggested that the class might sometime attempt a "Class Silence". This is best attempted during a period of relatively routine activity — perhaps a maths or gym lesson — when children will require to communicate with each other and the teacher. We suggest that, for sanity's sake, the teacher does not join in!

The first activity in the section on the importance and function of written language is discussion of a picture in which written language is used for various purposes, e.g.
> to inform
> to disseminate information to many people
> to record specific information for reference over time
> to aid short-term memory
> to entertain
> to communicate over distance.

BOOK TWO

Children are asked to identify all the samples of written language and to describe their functions. Again, categorisation by function may prove difficult, and teachers may have to help children put their ideas into words. The next discussion topic (various people's need for written language) gives an opportunity for thinking further about these functional categories.

There are no written exercises to accompany this chapter.

> **Vocabulary**
> *Revises:* spoken language, written language.

CHAPTER 2
Common and Proper Nouns

The concept of the noun was first introduced in Book One. A definition is given here and revision material is presented in the form of the game "Alphabetical Shopkeepers", which also leads on to the next concept. Teachers should, of course, add to this revision if necessary, perhaps by referring back to Book One, Chapter 3, and playing some of the games suggested there.

Proper nouns were also introduced in Book One. Here we provide an opportunity for children to work out the difference between common and proper nouns, from the study of examples of both. We suggest that teachers should allow plenty of time for children to look at the examples, and plenty of time for discussion of the difference. Children will be hampered by lack of vocabulary, and may have acquired a good concept of proper nouns without being able to express it verbally. When the time comes to help out, or to sum up, the following definitions are used throughout this course:

> A *noun* is the name of a person, place or thing.
> A *proper noun* is the special name of a particular person, place or thing.
> *Common nouns* are the general names for persons, places or things.

These definitions are necessary before children progress to the blackboard work on page 12.

Once work on this chapter has been completed, it is hoped that both teacher and pupils will benefit from using the technical vocabulary (proper noun, common noun) in discussing the punctuation of pupils' own written work.

The blackboard work carried out in the chapter should be erased before children begin the exercises.

Answers to Exercises *pages 14–16 pupil's book*

Common and Proper Nouns

A   A *noun* is the name of a *person*, *place* or *thing*. *Common nouns* refer to *persons/people*, *places* or *things* in general. They begin with small letters. *Proper* nouns are special names for particular examples of *persons/people, places and things*. They begin with *capital* letters.

B Form filled in for each individual:

A Form About Me
My forename: _____

My surname: _____

My address: _____

_____

My school: _____

My birth month: _____

My pets' names (if none, write "None"): _____

My favourite day of the week: _____

C 1) Columns containing ten proper nouns on the left, and ten equivalent common nouns on the right.

2) Columns containing ten proper nouns on the left, and ten equivalent common nouns on the right.

D 1) <u>Sarah</u> and <u>Marie</u> gave the (book) to the (teacher).

2) The (baker) sold (bread) (cakes) and (biscuits).

3) <u>Frankenstein</u> made a (monster) in his (laboratory).

E 1) Mr. Jenkins always goes to France for his holidays.
2) The name of Francis Drake's ship was *The Golden Hind*.
3) *Black Beauty* is a book by Anna Sewell.
4) Celtic and Rangers are football teams in Glasgow.

Vocabulary
Revises: noun, proper noun, forename, surname.
Introduces: common noun.

CHAPTER 3
Verbs and Sentences

The verb was introduced in Book One as a "doing word". It is reintroduced here, through activity, as a *word of doing or being*. Teachers should ensure that pupils have a good concept of the term "verb" before continuing beyond this definition in the text. If pupils are uncertain, it may be worthwhile revising Chapter 6 of *Mind Your Language*, Book One.

The chapter also reintroduces the terms "sentence" and "phrase", which were first defined in Book One, Chapter 7. The key concept here is that "every sentence contains a verb". The teacher may wish to provide further examples of sentences on

BOOK TWO

the blackboard for "Spot the Verb" activities. At this stage, it is advisable to stick to fairly obvious verbs — bona fide "doing words" like jump, swim, etc. — which pupils will find easy to identify.

The Verb TO BE
We have redefined verbs as "words of doing or being" because the most commonly used verb is "to be", and many other verbs relate to states rather than actions (e.g. "to become", "to remain", "to belong"). Here we give an opportunity to look at familiar parts of the verb "to be", so that pupils may recognise these henceforth as verbs — am, is, was, will be, used to be, were.

Pupils are invited to write these on the board, and then to contribute any other parts of the verb "to be" that they can think of. This is very difficult, and only extremely able children are likely to be successful. They may, with luck, think of other verb-groups such as "has been", "have been", "shall be", "shall have been", etc.

But the outstanding missing part is *"are"*. The teacher may be able to guide pupils towards this, or may prefer to supply it him/herself, depending on how well this section of the chapter has gone so far. However, although most children of 8+ will probably find it difficult to supply parts of the verb "to be", they are likely to have enough intuitive grasp of the language to recognise these parts as members of the same verbal family. Once it has been pointed out to them that "is", "was", etc., are verbs, the majority of children of this age should be able to recognise them in this capacity in a sentence.

The final activity requires pupils to "spot the verb" in a number of sentences, and revises the punctuation of sentences. This activity can then be extended to the pupils' own work — underlining verbs and verb-groups in sentences they have specially written themselves — as is suggested in Exercise D. However, it is not recommended that the activity be tried out on samples of language drawn from the children's own reading material — such material will probably contain many complex sentences, which may confuse children at this point.

Answers to Exercises *pages 21–22 pupil's book*

Verbs and Sentences

A A verb is a word of *doing* or *being*. Every sentence contains a *verb*. If a group of words does not have a verb it is not a *sentence*. It is called a *phrase*.
One very common verb is the verb *to be*.

B 1) There are *eight* sentences in the story.
2) We show a new sentence is starting with a *capital letter*.
3) We show the end of a sentence with a *full stop*.
4) Each sentence in the story has one verb. The verbs in the story are *was, was, ate, were, gobbled, was, ate, grew*.

C Three sentences copied from the box on page 19. All parts of verb "to be" underlined.

D 1) Most animals <u>run</u> away from their enemies.
2) An octopus <u>sprays</u> ink at its enemies.
3) A hedgehog <u>rolls</u> up in a ball.
4) A skunk <u>makes</u> a horrible smell.

E Three sentences about the child's own activities last night. All verbs should be underlined.

> **Vocabulary**
> *Revises:* verb, verb-group, sentence, capital letter, full stop, phrase.
> *Introduces:* the verb TO BE.

CHAPTER 4
Adjectives: Making Sentences Grow

The chapter begins with brief revision of nouns and verbs. Pupils are expected by this stage to be familiar with both these terms and able to identify both parts of speech.

The adjective was introduced in Book One, Chapter 9. If pupils require revision of the concept, we suggest that the teacher refers back to this chapter and perhaps plays the "Adjective Superhero" game before continuing.

The definition of an adjective offered throughout this course is "an adjective describes a noun".

The chapter investigates the use of adjectives to make sentences "more interesting". Simple sentences composed of nouns and verbs (and determiners, "the" or "a") are expanded by the introduction of suitable adjectives. Pupils are also asked to reverse the process — reducing sentences to nouns and verbs (and determiners).

These techniques of expansion and reduction are important types of sentence transformation. They show how a basic sentence structure underlies a more complex-looking finished product. This point is not made explicitly in the chapter, as it is considered a little difficult for children at this stage. However, it is hoped that by manipulating language in this way children will gradually become aware of the significance of expansion and reduction. The activity "Word Identikit" uses the same technique to demonstrate how one basic sentence structure can be embellished in a multitude of different ways.

After pupils have completed this chapter, teachers may consider it an appropriate time for creative writing activities concentrating on the use of adjectives to improve a piece of writing.

Answers to Exercises *pages 26–27 pupil's book*

Making Sentences More Interesting

A Every sentence has a *verb*. Some simple sentences are made up of just the *verb* and some *nouns*. We can make sentences more interesting by adding *adjectives* to describe the *nouns*.

B 1) A <u>beautiful</u> |woman| (sang) a <u>short</u> <u>sad</u> |song|.

2) The <u>little</u> |girl| (ate) the <u>sour</u> <u>green</u> |apple|.

3) The <u>huge</u> <u>hairy</u> |monster| (destroyed) the <u>old</u> |city|.

4) The <u>little</u> |dog| (ate) the <u>big</u> <u>juicy</u> |bone|.

BOOK TWO

    5) A <u>young</u> |policeman| (chased) the <u>fat</u> |robber|.

    6) A <u>white-faced, red-nosed</u> |clown| (threw) a <u>big yellow</u> |pie|.

C 1) A woman sang a song.
    2) The girl ate the apple.
    3) The monster destroyed the city.
    4) The dog ate the bone.
    5) A policeman chased the robber.
    6) A clown threw a pie.

D The following sentences with adjectives added:
    1) The   man ate the   sandwich.
    2) The   cat climbed the   tree.
    3) A   girl jumped out of the   car.

E A description of a woman, using adjectives from the Word Identikit activity. Basic sentence reads:
    The woman had eyes and a nose. She had a mouth.
    She was wearing a dress and a coat.

> **Vocabulary**
> *Revises:* noun, verb, adjective.

CHAPTER 5
Parts of Speech: Pronouns

This chapter first introduces the term "parts of speech" to describe nouns, verbs and adjectives. It is assumed that pupils will by now have a sufficient understanding of these specific parts of speech to accept a generic term to embrace them all.

    The final part of speech to be covered in Book Two of *Mind Your Language* is the pronoun. The definition we give is "a pronoun stands in place of a noun", and this is illustrated by substituting appropriate nouns in parts of sentences where pronouns would usually stand. As intuitive users of the language, children of 8+ are aware that this is "incorrect" and can provide a "correct" version. The teacher may wish to give more examples of noun/pronoun substitution (as in the box on page 28) if he/she considers more practice is required.

    Pupils are also asked to substitute nouns for pronouns (changing "correct" to "incorrect" versions). This is more difficult, and again further examples may be necessary to give sufficient practice.

    The next activity is the placing of pronouns in columns depending on whether they are first, second or third person. Children are invited to come out and write pronouns on the board, selecting the appropriate column. We suggest that, as each pronoun is written, the teacher asks the rest of the class to put thumbs up or down, depending on whether it is in the correct column. This involves all the children throughout the activity and should give the teacher an idea of who has grasped the concept of "person" and who hasn't. Some children should gradually come to internalise the concept throughout the activity.

BOOK TWO

The final activity, "Ban the Pronoun", may be difficult for less able children, so we suggest that they be paired with children likely to succeed, who can provide a model for them. The columns of pronouns on the blackboard should be erased before pupils begin the written exercises. We ask them to repeat this activity individually, to give each child the chance to categorise by person.

Answers to Exercises *pages 32–33 pupil's book*

Parts of Speech — Pronouns

A Nouns, verbs and adjectives are called *parts* of *speech*. These different sorts of words do different jobs in a sentence. Another *part* of *speech* is the pronoun. A *pronoun* stands in place of a *noun*.

B

First Person Pronouns	Second Person Pronouns	Third Person Pronouns	
I	you	his	itself
me	yourself	he	them
my	yours	him	they
myself	yourselves	himself	their
mine	your	she	theirs
we		her	themselves
us		hers	
our		herself	
ourselves		it	
ours		its	

C 1) The king wore *his* crown.
2) The children came into school. Then *they* sat down.
3) Pick up your pen and put *it* in the pencil case.
4) Beth feeds *her* goldfish every day.
5) We write *our* names inside *our* wellies so they won't get mixed up.
NB. If children have written other pronouns which nonetheless make sense, they should, of course, be marked correct.

D 1) The boy ran as fast as *he* could. *He* was trying to win the race. *It* was an important one, and *he* had been training hard for *it*.
2) Steve and Sally went to the shops. *They* bought some sweets. Steve ate all *his* sweets, but Sally saved *hers* till *they* got home. Then *she* ate *them/hers*.
3) My brother and I are going to visit our gran. *We* like going to see *her*. *She* gives *us* cakes for tea.

E Passage copied from reading book: nouns substituted for all pronouns.

> **Vocabulary**
> *Revises:* noun, verb, adjective.
> *Introduces:* part of speech, pronoun.

CHAPTER 6
Sentences and Subjects

This chapter begins the course work on sentence structure, with the introduction of the term "the subject". Every sentence has a subject and a verb, and the simplest English sentence structure is subject + verb (an SV sentence).

We introduce "the subject" by providing eight sentences (in which pupils are asked to identify the verbs) and then we list the subjects of these sentences. Pupils are then asked to look at these examples and puzzle out what "the subject" is and some rules of thumb about its position in a sentence, etc. It is up to the teacher to guide discussion here, and difficult to be precise. Statements like "the subject is the who or what that *does* the verb" or "the subject is the actor" give a general idea, but no definition can be completely satisfactory for children of this age.

The children will probably note that the subject comes immediately *before* the verb in all our examples — and, as this is usually the case in the simple sentence structures they will meet at this stage, we are happy for them to accept it for now. (However, don't be dogmatic about this: children may notice exceptions, e.g. "Can Jane swim?", "No," said Jane.) We have tried to show (in examples 4 and 7) that the subject does not necessarily come at the very beginning of a sentence.

As for parts of speech, the subjects of our sentences are nouns, noun phrases (e.g. determiner + adjective + noun) or pronouns standing for nouns. They are always people, places or things.

However, pupils' specific answers to the questions we have set are not particularly important. What is important is that they should look at the sample sentences and come to some intuitive understanding of the relationship between subject and verb: the questions merely provide a reason for looking.

We hope that the discussion will help pupils to conceptualise something like this:

SUBJECT	VERB
someone something somewhere	does/is

Thereafter, we try to guide pupils to identify subject and verb by
  1) finding the verb
  2) working out who/what does/is the verb (subject).
Throughout the course subjects and verb are shown thus:

S   V
The teacher despaired.

Work in the rest of the chapter is aimed at
  1) giving practice in identification/manipulation of subjects and verbs;
  2) investigating the *reduction* of sentences to a subject+verb base.

Answers to Exercises *pages 39–40 pupil's book*

Sentences and Subjects

A Every sentence has a *subject*. The *subject* goes with the *verb* and is usually found just in front of the *verb*. Some very simple sentences are made up of just a *subject* and a *verb*.

B
1) The plane (S) flew (V) over the city.
2) Rabbits (S) eat (V) grass and other plants.
3) The guard (S) checks (V) the tickets on a train.
4) Penguins (S) live (V) near the South Pole.
5) Babies (S) cry (V).
6) We (S) come (V) to school on weekdays.
7) At weekends, we (S) stay (V) at home.

C
1) Jack and Jill (S) ......
2) Little Bo Peep (S) ......
3) Little Jack Horner (S) ......
4) My best friend (S) ......
5) I (S) ......

+ verb and suitable sentence-ending in each case.

D
1) ...... had (V) a little lamb
2) Suitable ...... jumped (V) over the moon
3) subjects ...... ran (V) up the clock.
4) ...... is (V) the fastest runner in our class.
5) ...... is (V) my favourite colour.

E The following sentences expanded by the addition of further detail:
1) The dog barked.
2) I sang.
3) The girl ran.
4) The moon rose.
5) Ducks swim.

Vocabulary
Revises: sentence, verb, noun, pronoun.
Introduces: subject.

CHAPTER 7
Punctuation: Making Sense with Sentences

This chapter introduces the punctuation of continuous text — at present concentrating on the marking of sentences by full stops and capital letters. As in previous chapters on punctuation (Book One), we suggest that punctuation marks in written language fulfil the same function as pauses, tonal variation and facial expression in spoken language: they help to organise the language into "chunks", thus clarifying the meaning for the reader or listener. To make this point we use the idea of uninflected, continuous "computer-speak", where a robot-like delivery of spoken language impedes the sense. This is represented in written language by a continuous, unpunctuated text.

Pupils are asked how this "computer-speak" differs from human speech, and it is worthwhile allowing the class a little time for investigation and discussion of this. (If possible, listening to a tape of normal adult conversation may be of help in alerting them to spoken language techniques.)

Teachers often explain punctuation of sentences in terms of "pausing for breath", (e.g. "You put a full stop where you pause for breath at the end of a sentence"), but this is not always true. In normal conversation, speakers often pause and hesitate more *within* sentences than at sentence boundaries. Spoken language patterns are highly complex: inflections, pauses, speed of delivery and much non-linguistic information all combine to aid "chunking" of the message.

The key point is that, no matter how the "chunks" are achieved in each speech act, they are *meaningful* units of language. It is the *sense* of the message which determines its delivery. We use our voices, faces and gestures to help make language make sense.

Similarly, in written language we use punctuation marks to "chunk" a text into meaningful units, thus guiding our readers to the sense of the message. In the incorrectly punctuated version of Frankie's message, full stops and capital letters do *not* help the language make sense — indeed, they impede the sense.

We do not expect children to come to any firm conclusions about how spoken and written language are punctuated (indeed, linguists and philosophers are still arguing about it!); we merely hope that discussion of the question will alert them to this facet of language, making them aware of the importance of "chunking for meaning". We also hope that, as a result of the work in this chapter, teacher and pupils may have a shared linguistic awareness and a larger technical vocabulary on which to draw when discussing individual pupils' punctuation of their own continuous prose.

Answers to Exercises *page 45 pupil's book*

Sense and Sentences

A A *sentence* is a group of words that make *sense* on their own. Every *sentence* has a *subject* and a *verb*. We break up our writing into *sentences* to help our readers understand what we mean. We use *punctuation* marks to show where sentences begin and end. A *full stop* shows the end of a *sentence*. A *capital letter* shows that a new *sentence* is beginning.

B Once upon a time there was a teddy bear who worked on a building site.

He used to dig holes with a pick. One day he came back from his lunch and found that his pick had been stolen. That was the day the teddy bear had his pick nicked.

Once there was a man who slept with his head under a pillow. One day this man woke up without any teeth. The fairies had taken them away.

D Here is the news. This afternoon a train carrying jelly crashed with a train carrying fresh cream. Police say that rail services will be running a trifle late. On the MI a lorry has spilt a load of hair restorer. Police are combing the area. Finally we have news of the man who stole a calendar. He got twelve months.

> **Vocabulary**
> *Revises:* sentence, full stop, capital letter, subject, verb.

CHAPTER 8
Punctuation: Using Punctuation Marks

The question mark and exclamation mark were introduced in Book One, Chapters 5 and 8. They are reintroduced here in a continuation of the work on voice-tone and punctuation which was begun in the preceding chapter. In Book One we described the exclamation mark as showing a "raised voice"; we now suggest that it can also be used to show that someone is making a joke or that words are "not meant to be taken seriously".

The discussion material at the beginning of the chapter and the "Gobbledegook" activity are intended to alert children to variations in tone and expression in speech, and to representation of some of these variations by different punctuation marks.

The question mark and exclamation mark are treated as "specialised full stops", which help both to "chunk" language into meaningful units and to indicate something about the tone in which these units of language should be read.

The Comma
The second part of the chapter relates to the comma, which is used to help with the internal organisation of sentences. We suggest that pupils should not yet attempt to use commas in their own writing, except in one context — the separating of items in a list. However, they should by now be paying attention to punctuation in their *reading*, to help in establishing the meaning intended by the author of a text. Teachers can encourage this by directing attention to punctuation during reading sessions.

Answers to Exercises *pages 52–53 pupil's book*

Punctuation Marks and the Comma

A *Punctuation marks* break up what we write into *sentences* that make *sense*. A *question mark* shows that a sentence should be read in a questioning voice. An *exclamation mark* shows that a sentence should be read in a raised voice. It can also show that someone is joking.

B 1) Where is my dinner?
2) Don't do that. (or) Don't do that!
3) Cotton comes from a plant grown in warm countries.
4) It is very cold at the North Pole.
5) How far is it to your house?
6) Help! — I'm stuck in a tree! (Or other suitable punctuation)

C A *comma* is another *punctuation mark*. It looks like a *full stop* with a little tail. It is used to separate the items in a *list*. It can also show short breaks inside *sentences*.

D 1) I like playing football, cricket, tennis and rounders.
2) The spoilt little boy cried, screamed, kicked and spat.
3) The witch had a long, thin, knobbly nose.
(or) The witch had a long thin knobbly nose.
4) On holiday we sat on the beach, swam in the sea, went on the pier and spent a day at the fairground.

E 1) Cakes are made with flour, eggs, butter and milk.
2) At the zoo they had huge grey elephants, sweet little lion cubs, two-humped camels and a giraffe.
3) The four longest rivers in the world are the Nile, the Amazon, the Yangtze-Kiang and the Lena.
4) At school we write stories, draw pictures, read books and work out maths problems.

F 1) Dentist: Have your teeth ever been checked?
Patient: No, they've always been white.
2) Doctor: How did your feet get so badly scalded?
Patient: I was making soup for my tea.
Doctor: Did you spill it?
Patient: No, I just followed the instructions on the tin.
Doctor: What did it say on the tin?
Patient: Stand in hot water for ten minutes.

> **Vocabulary**
> *Revises:* sentence, full stop, capital letter,
> question mark, exclamation mark.
> *Introduces:* statement, comma, tone of voice,
> expression.

CHAPTER 9
Punctuation: The Apostrophe

The apostrophe is an exception among punctuation marks in that it does not provide a guide as to how sentences should be read. We point out in this chapter that it is found *inside* words, either to show ownership (see Book Four) or to show contraction. This chapter deals with the latter use of the apostrophe.

The work suggested is quite straightforward, the point to be emphasized being that the apostrophe is inserted *where letters have been omitted* in a contraction. We recommend that pupils write up all the examples on the blackboard, as suggested in the text, and are given time and encouragement to work out this rule for the insertion of apostrophes.

Contracted words are a feature of spoken language, and the apostrophe allows this feature to be represented in writing. However, in formal written language it is still usually considered correct to avoid contractions, except in the representation of direct speech. This distinction would probably be lost on most pupils of 8+, who are still writing "spoken language". However, able children who have achieved a higher degree of literacy may benefit from discussion of this question.

Answers to Exercises *pages 57–58 pupil's book*

The Apostrophe in Shortened Words

A The apostrophe is a *punctuation mark* which is found inside *words*. It can show that *letters* have been missed out of a word. This often happens when two words are pushed together. The *apostrophe* goes where the letter or letters are *missed out/missing/missed*.

B I'll = I (sha)ll   haven't = have n(o)t
you've = you (ha)ve   it'd = it (woul)d
she's = she (i)s   could've = could (ha)ve
it's = it (i)s   we're = we (a)re
wouldn't = would n(o)t   wasn't = was n(o)t
isn't = is n(o)t   they're = they (a)re
mustn't = must n(o)t   they've = they (ha)ve
I'm = I (a)m   o'clock = o(f the) clock

C 1) I'd like to come but I can't.
2) They've just got back from their holidays.
3) It's raining today. It'll probably rain tomorrow too.
4) You mustn't do that — it's dangerous.
5) People who live in glass houses shouldn't throw stones.

D 1) It's too cold to play out.
2) We're looking forward to the party.
3) Don't stop writing till you've finished the page.
4) I've read all these books, haven't I?
5) Your mother says you'll have to pay for the broken window.

E Emma: What has got a lot of legs, pink eyes, yellow wings and a striped black body?
Tim: I don't know. What is it?
Emma: I don't know either, but it's crawling up the back of your neck.

> **Vocabulary**
> *Revises:* punctuation marks.
> *Introduces:* apostrophe.

CHAPTER 10
Spoken Language versus Written Language

As we stated in the notes to Book Two, Chapter 1, an understanding of the essential differences between spoken and written language is necessary before a child can acquire complete literacy. In Chapter 1 we tried to alert children to the importance of language in our lives, looking first at spoken language and then at written language.

This final chapter provides discussion material and activities which deliberately compare and contrast the two types of language. We aim to make children more aware of these two types by pointing to specific differences in:

    a) the *production* of spoken and written language (hopefully, children will remember the work covered in Chapters 7 and 8);

    b) the *uses* of spoken and written language.

Teachers should use the discussion questions merely as a basis for discussion — further reasons for opinions can be sought, and examples requested, etc. Children may have anecdotes to relate (some of them relevant!), or questions which may be investigated.

The most obvious use of written language is as an aide-mémoire (both classroom activities indicate this), but teachers may find ways of directing discussion to cover the other main uses listed in the notes to Chapter 1 (see page 21). For this reason, it will probably be well worth ensuring that the children complete the final activity "Why Was It Written Down?", as it should produce much useful data for discussion.

There are no exercises to accompany this chapter.

Vocabulary

Revises: written language, spoken language.

BOOK THREE

CHAPTER 1
Parts of Speech: Nouns, Verbs, Adjectives

In this first chapter of Book Three we reintroduce three parts of speech — nouns, verbs and adjectives. These have been comprehensively covered in previous books, and pupils who have covered the *Mind Your Language* course so far should be adequately familiar with them. However, teachers who feel it necessary to provide revision activities may wish to use the games and activities suggested in Book One (Chapters 3, 6 and 9) to ensure that the concepts are thoroughly understood.

The chapter makes the point that many words can function as more than one part of speech. "Train" for instance, may be a noun (a railway train) or a verb (to train an animal). Consideration of this facet of language gives opportunities for development of the following aspects of linguistic awareness:
  1) increasing objective awareness of words, as operating in various ways within a rational system;
  2) use of *metalinguistic* terms (technical language, such as "verb" and "noun") to discuss how language is used.

Children of 9+ who are linguistically able will probably find it quite easy to recognise and define how a word is being used in a sentence, and to switch usage from one part of speech to another. Other children, however, may be able to make such adjustments only intuitively: they will find it difficult to define exactly what is going on when a word is used first, say, as a noun and then as a verb. The suggested methods of checking how a word is being used (given on page 7) may be of particular help to such children, and it is recommended that plenty of time and help be given to achieve understanding of the checking methods.

A useful follow-up activity in spelling is consideration of the different spelling of certain words depending on whether they are used nominally or verbally:

Noun	**Verb**
practice	practise
licence	license
advice	advise

Answers to Exercises *pages 8–9 pupil's book*

Parts of Speech

A A noun is the name of a person, place or thing. (Or any other suitable definition.)
   A verb is a word of doing or being. "
   An adjective describes a noun. "

B *Nouns*, *verbs* and *adjectives* are all parts of speech. Some words can be used as more than one *part* of *speech*. You have to check the job a word is doing in a sentence to decide what *part* of *speech* it is.

35

BOOK THREE

C I shall *ring* you tonight. (VERB)
She wore a diamond *ring* on her finger. (NOUN)
He took some *paper* from the desk. (NOUN)
At the party we wore *paper* hats. (ADJECTIVE)
The boy *coloured* his picture. (VERB)
There were some *coloured* balls on the pool table. (ADJECTIVE)
The soldier *fires* his gun. (VERB)
The firemen put out the *fires* with hoses. (NOUN)

D old, beautiful, little, sad, angry.

E Two sentences for each of these words, one using the word nominally, one using it verbally:
swing, brush, trip, record.

> **Vocabulary**
> *Revises:* part of speech, noun, verb, adjective.

CHAPTER 2
Tense: Past, Present, Future

Chapter 2 introduces the concept of tense. Children of 9+ are capable of selecting and producing the correct tenses of verbs in their speech (and usually in their writing), but often are unaware that they are doing so. The concepts of "past", "present" and "future" must therefore be clarified before tense is discussed.

There are various ways of forming each tense, e.g.:

Past	**Present**	**Future**
I walked	I walk	I shall walk
I was walking	I am walking	I am going to walk
I have walked		
I used to walk		

Any of these is acceptable in response to the discussion questions, and children should be encouraged to notice that a variety of forms exist. There is, however, no need to introduce the technical terms (e.g. past imperfect) to describe them.

Children's understanding of the concept of tense should be of help to the teacher when discussing individuals' personal writing: a common error at this stage is that of slipping from one tense to another.

The final discussion point before the activity relates to the tense in which fiction is usually written. It refers children to the class library to check. Usually, of course, novels are written in the past tense (although some children may notice that direct speech is in the present). Teachers may wish to draw the attention of able pupils to the occasional use of the present tense throughout a novel, by authors such as Gene Kemp (*The Turbulent Term of Tyke Tiler* and *Gowie Corbie Plays Chicken*), Clive King (*Me and My Million*) and Betsy Byars (*Cracker Jackson*). Consideration of the reasons behind the selection of the present tense may provide interesting discussion material.

BOOK THREE

Answers to Exercises *pages 14–15 pupil's book*

Verbs and Tense

A Every verb has a tense. The tense of a *verb* tells you when it happens — in the *past*, the *present* or the *future*.

B

Past	Present	Future
last Friday	now	next week
when I was a baby	at the moment	when I'm twenty-one
		a week on Monday

C
1) In 1492 Columbus <u>sailed</u> to America.
2) One day, people <u>will visit</u> other planets.
3) Jesus <u>lived</u> about 2,000 years ago.
4) I <u>am writing</u> this at school.
5) After school I <u>shall go</u> home.
6) At the moment, we <u>are working</u> in our language books.

D
1) (**PA**)
2) (**F**)
3) (**PA**)
4) (**PR**)
5) (**F**)
6) (**PR**)

E
1) Passage to be written in *future* tense: variation from this model may occur.
James *will go* to the park at the weekend. He *will play* football with his friends and *he will enjoy* the game. At five o'clock his mother *will pick* him up in the car. They *will go* home for tea.
2) Passage to be written in *present* tense:
Penny *likes* wearing jeans. Her mother *is* always telling her to wear something smarter. But Penny *thinks* her jeans *are* smart. She *feels* good in them.
3) Passage to be written in the *past* tense:
The space traveller *arrived* on the unknown planet. He *landed* his space-ship and *took* his first steps on the new land. He *explored* the planet carefully, and *reported* back to base.

F Two passages in the *present* tense: variation from the models may occur:
1) James *goes* to the park at the weekend. He *plays* football with his friends and *enjoys* the game. At five o'clock his mother *picks* him up in the car. They *go* home for tea.
2) The space traveller *arrives* on the unknown planet. He *lands* his space-ship and *takes* his first steps on the new land. He *explores* the planet carefully, and *reports* back to base.

Vocabulary
Revises: verbs.
Introduces: tense, past, present, future.

BOOK THREE

CHAPTER 3
Nouns and Pronouns: Singular and Plural

The concepts of singularity and plurality are well understood by children of 9+, although the terminology used may be unfamiliar. The chapter, therefore, provides numerous opportunities for the use of the terms "singular" and "plural" in context, while revising nouns and, more particularly, pronouns.

Singular and Plural Nouns
We ask pupils to work out the rule for making regular plural nouns. We then look at English irregular plural nouns and the difficulties these present to the non-native speaker. (Pupils should be competent to produce most of these irregular plurals by now, but may be unaware that they *are* plurals, and doubtful of their connection to the singular noun.)

Singular and Plural Pronouns
Pronouns were introduced in Book Two, Chapter 5, and teachers may wish to ensure that this chapter has been covered before proceeding with the work here. We offer some brief revision of the function of pronouns at the beginning of the chapter.

The three categories, 1st person, 2nd person, and 3rd person, are presented, each containing ten pronouns. Five pronouns in each case are singular and five are plural, although this is not easy to see at first glance, as in some cases the words are identical (e.g. "you"-Singular Nominative and "you"-Plural Nominative). Pupils are asked to fit them into a grid, thus:

	Singular	Plural
1st person	I, me, my, mine, myself	we, us, our, ours, ourselves
2nd person	you, you, your, yours, yourself	you, you, your, yours, yourselves
3rd person	he/she/it, him/her/it, his/her/its, his/hers/its, himself/herself/itself	they, them, their, theirs, themselves

In each section of the grid, therefore, there are pronouns which would adequately fill the gaps in these sentences:
    ...... read(s) a book.
    Give the book to ......
    It is ...... book.
    The book is ......
    It was bought by ......

This activity is presented as a class or group activity, and some groups may need a lot of guidance. Teachers are advised to treat it (and the next activity, Pronoun Happy Families) fairly light-heartedly. It is not important that children should

know exactly how to categorise personal pronouns. The two activities are provided as:
- a) an opportunity for pupils to familiarise themselves with some commonly used pronouns;
- b) a demonstration of the three categories of "person" — I, you, he/she/it, and the equivalent plurals;
- c) a chance for more able children to recognise and perhaps internalise the categories of pronoun, for facilitation of second language learning.

Answers to Exercises *page 21 pupil's book*

Nouns and Pronouns — Singular and Plural

A Nouns and pronouns are all either *singular* or *plural*. *Singular* means one and *plural* means more than one.

B

Singular	Plural
dog	policemen
horse	matches
pencil	teeth
sausage	girls
mouse	chips

C 1) mice 2) men 3) children 4) sheep 5) geese 6) feet 7) deer 8) women

D
1) I put my glasses down and couldn't find *them* anywhere.
2) David signed *his* name with a flourish.
3) Deciduous trees lose *their* leaves in the winter.
4) Where did *you* go for your holidays?
5) When Helen was ready, *she* ran downstairs.

E See grid on previous page.

> **Vocabulary**
> *Revises:* noun, pronoun, 1st person, 2nd person, 3rd person.
> *Introduces:* singular, plural.

CHAPTER 4
Subject and Verb: Agreement

The concept of the *subject* was introduced in Book Two. Pupils were not provided with a definition, but were required to recognise the subject in a sentence, and to note its relationship to the verb. A short revision section is provided at the start of this chapter — if teachers feel it is not adequate for their pupils' needs, they may wish to look back to Book Two, Chapter 6, before proceeding with the work.

Every sentence contains a subject and a verb, and these two elements must *agree*.

BOOK THREE

Children of 9+ abide by this grammatical rule in their spoken language, and intuitively adjust verb-endings to make verbs agree with their subjects. They are not, however, conscious of doing this, and can therefore often make errors in written work, when they lose track of the subject before they get round to writing the verb. An understanding of the concept of "agreement" can make them more conscious of the rule in their written work. It is also useful for the teacher to know that his/her pupils share an understanding of the term "agreement" so that it can be used when discussing the pupils' own written language.

It is important to note, however, that some instances of apparent non-agreement of subject and verb in pupils' writing (and, indeed, in their speech) are due to dialect variation, rather than grammatical error. Some children will have learnt applications of, for instance, the verb "to be", which are different from those of Standard English, e.g. "The book were boring" or "We was just going". The question of dialect is covered in Book Four, Chapter 5, and the teacher may find it useful to consult this chapter to decide on the most suitable attitude to dialect variation. Our own position is to accept it, at this stage, as "correct" in spoken English, but to point out that in Standard English (in which we should write) it is considered "incorrect".

To introduce the topic of "agreement" in the chapter, we provide two groups of simple SV sentences in which the subjects are missing. In the first group, the verb-endings encourage the insertion of singular subjects, and in the second group, they expect plural subjects. We stress that the subjects must be nouns (the pronoun "you" could ruin the whole thing!), and we hope that teachers will ensure that acceptable subjects are inserted, to demonstrate the point.

The chapter goes on to point out that other parts of a sentence must also agree with the subject, e.g. pronouns. Pupils are given opportunities to change sentences from singular to plural, or from plural to singular. Teachers may wish to give further practice in this by providing more sentences of the same type.

Answers to Exercises *pages 28–29 pupil's book*

Subjects and Verbs — Agreement

A Every sentence has a *verb*. Every sentence also has a *subject*. The subject and verb always *agree*. So *verb*-endings are often different, depending on whether the *subject* is singular or *plural*. Sometimes other words in the sentences must *agree* with the subject too.

B
1) Isaac Newton (S) discovered (V) the law of gravity.
2) The Second World War (S) began (V) in 1939.
3) We (S) live (V) in Britain.
4) Usually, bears (S) sleep (V) all through the winter.
5) Paris (S) is (V) the capital of France.

C Suitable subjects inserted in the following sentences:
1) .... sells bread and cakes.

2) .... looks after people in hospital.
3) .... are wild animals with black and white coats.
4) .... fly in the sky.
5) .... wears a blue uniform.
6) .... is very intelligent.

D Changed from singular, e.g.:
1) The boys hang up their coats.
2) The dogs always take their bones into the garden(s).
3) We were late for school.
4) They were tying their shoelaces.
5) Our names were written inside our coats.

E Changed from plural, e.g.:
1) A badger lives in a sett.
2) The girl is having her dinner.
3) The teacher marks his/her pupil's (s') work.
4) The bird flies high in the sky.
5) A baby does not know how to talk.

> **Vocabulary**
> *Revises:* verb, subject, singular, plural.
> *Introduces:* agreement.

CHAPTER 5
Parts of Speech: Adverbs

The adverb is the final part of speech to be introduced in the series. We relate it to the adjective, as both parts of speech have a descriptive function — the definition of adverb used throughout the series is "An adverb tells you more about a verb".

Two types of adverb are introduced: *adverbs of manner* and *adverbs of time*. It is important that pupils develop a good concept of the former before progressing to the work on the latter. Teachers may prefer to tackle the chapter in two parts, with a break after the activity "The Adverb Game".

As in previous chapters about parts of speech, we provide material through which pupils may work out the function of adverbs (of manner) for themselves. And again, we stress that the more time teachers are prepared to devote to this activity, the greater the likelihood that pupils will acquire a good understanding of the concept. They may not be able to verbalise this understanding particularly well, but consideration of the examples gives an opportunity for *active* mental processing of language, which is more valuable than the passive reception of a definition. This definition is provided later in the text, and pupils can match their own attempts against it. The activity, "The Adverb Game", helps reinforce the concept, and, once the rules have been acquired, it can be played whenever the class has ten minutes to spare.

Adverbs of manner are defined as answering the question "How?" and adverbs of time as answering the question "When?" The latter are slightly more difficult to spot, and teachers should not be too concerned if the less able members of a class

BOOK THREE

are unsure about them. We recommend that a poster of adverbs of time is compiled to help with their identification.

The work on adverbs of time is linked with *tense* to provide an opportunity for revision of the topic.

Answers to Exercises *pages 33–34 pupil's book*

Parts of Speech — Adverbs

A An *adverb* tells you more about a *verb*. An *adverb* of *manner* answers the question "how?" An *adverb* of *time* answers the question "when?".

B
1) The girl <u>trudged</u> (sadly) to school but <u>skipped</u> (happily) home.
2) I <u>looked</u> (hopefully) at the letter.
3) (Fiercely) the dog <u>growled</u> at the burglar.
4) The boy <u>shouted</u> as (loudly) as he could.
5) The children <u>filed</u> (silently) into the hall and the headmaster <u>watched</u> them (sternly).

C Suitable adverbs of manner in the spaces:
1) Jamie sings ....
2) Our teacher smiles .... at the class.
3) I do my homework ....
4) My friend dances ....
5) My dad tells me to go to bed ....

D
1) We <u>will see</u> the doctor (soon).
2) (Today) I <u>am having</u> school dinners.
3) (Tomorrow) I <u>will bring</u> a packed lunch.
4) The vicar (always) <u>smiles</u> at us.
5) You (never) <u>write</u> neatly.

E Suitable adverbs of time in the spaces:
1) He will be coming home ....
2) .... I ripped my coat.
3) I am wearing my best clothes ....
4) It will .... be the weekend.
5) Mum .... gives me beans for tea.

> **Vocabulary**
> *Revises:* verb, adjective, tense.
> *Introduces:* adverb of manner, adverb of time.

CHAPTER 6
Punctuation Marks

In previous chapters, we have introduced punctuation marks as the written equivalents of various spoken language techniques for helping to imbue groups of words with *meaning*. In speech, intonation and pauses are used to break language up into meaningful "chunks": in writing, full stops and commas are used for this function. In speech, tone and expression — vocal and facial — give further indications of the intended meaning (e.g. whether the statement is a question, a command, a joke, a warning, etc.): in writing, the question mark and exclamation mark can give some indication of these variations.

This chapter opens with activities and discussion questions intended to remind pupils of variations in the delivery of spoken language and the equivalent punctuation in written language. It then goes on to look at examples of how different uses of a punctuation mark (the full stop) can change the meaning of a piece of writing, by "chunking" it differently.

Some uses of the comma

The comma was introduced in Book Two (Chapter 8), but the only function noted was that of separating the items in a list. Brief revision of this function is given here — teachers may prefer to provide further examples and practice before proceeding.

We then give a number of examples of spoken language, translated into speech bubbles, where commas represent specific breaks in the delivery. Pupils are invited to render these speeches correctly aloud, using the punctuation for guidance. We suggest that more able readers are selected to do this, as they are more likely to respond intuitively to the punctuation, and that each "playlet" should be read several times. Pupils are then asked, in pairs, to work out "rules" for the use of the comma in these examples.

We provide a list of four uses of the comma on page 67, with which pupils can eventually compare their own responses. In general, the examples illustrate the use of commas to separate the main content-bearing part of a sentence from short "tag" phrases, which are expendable to the sense of the message. Whether or not pupils "discover" this, the opportunity to look closely at and discuss the use of the comma should be of help in developing their own use of punctuation.

The "Talking Punctuation" activity which concludes the chapter is also very useful for sensitising pupils to the use of punctuation. However, it is usually helpful if pupils practise the noises before producing them as sound effects with the passages. The teacher can draw the punctuation marks on the blackboard and point to them to elicit the correct noises: when pupils are proficient at this, they can progress to the activity. "Talking Punctuation" can then be applied to other passages whenever an odd few minutes are available.

Answers to Exercises *pages 40–41 pupil's book*

Punctuation Marks

A *Punctuation marks* can show the tone of voice in which you should read a sentence. A *question mark* at the end of a sentence shows it is a *question*. A *full stop* shows an ordinary sentence. An *exclamation mark* shows that the sentence is to be said in a raised voice, or that it is not to be taken seriously.

Punctuation marks also show where breaks in the sense of a passage occur. A *full stop* shows the end of a sentence — a strong break. A *comma* shows a weaker break within a sentence.

B *Punctuation of sentences*
Suitable punctuation, which may differ from the models given here:
1) Where do you live?
2) Help!
3) Who lives in Buckingham Palace?
4) Matthew and Sam are playing in the park.
5) Stop that noise at once!
6) Look out!
7) Is it far from here to London?

C *The comma*
Suitable punctuation, which may differ from the models given here:
1) Mum, where is my schoolbag?
2) It's getting quite late, isn't it?
3) The colours of the rainbow are red, orange, yellow, green, blue, indigo and violet.
4) Well, Johnny, this is a terrible piece of work, isn't it?
5) Are you coming, Nancy?
6) Oh dear, I think I've forgotten my glasses.
7) No, I put them in my pocket, didn't I?
8) You've got cheese, ham and tomato sandwiches, haven't you?

D Passage copied from book without punctuation, and punctuated by another child. This should have been marked and discussed by the children involved.

> **Vocabulary**
> *Revises:* punctuation marks, full stop,
> capital letter, question mark,
> exclamation mark, comma, sentence.

CHAPTER 7
Speaking and Writing: Clear Enough?

As has been stressed in the chapters on punctuation, one of the most important factors in linguistic awareness is a recognition of the differences between spoken and written language. Spoken language is, to a large extent, *embedded* in the situation in which it occurs. As we have seen, tone of voice and facial expression contribute to the meaning of spoken language. So too do the physical circumstances in which speech is taking place. Speaker and hearer share an environment in time and space: a speaker can therefore expect his audience to understand inexplicit references to factors of that shared environment, using gesture and other non-verbal methods of communication to make his meaning clear. He can also see from that audience's responses whether his words are being fully understood, and adjust his language as necessary.

On the other hand, a writer and his audience may share no common background at all, and there is certainly no feedback to the writer as to whether his words are being understood. It is therefore much more important that the writer should be *explicit* in what he is trying to communicate. Details and descriptions which are unnecessary in spoken language are essential in written language, in order that the message may be understood.

In this chapter we introduce children to this idea, concentrating particularly on the need for more specific reference in written language (nouns rather than pronouns). [In Book Four, Chapter 4, the concept is tackled again, and other factors (the need for more descriptive material, etc.) are discussed.] We provide a number of examples of "spoken language written down", where the information provided is inadequate for a distant audience's comprehension. The examples include *instructions*, *narrative*, and *report-writing*, and pupils are asked to expand each piece to make it explicit and intelligible to a reader. Teachers should encourage discussion of each piece, eliciting a number of possible "rewrites" and allowing the class to deliberate between them, rather than accepting the first one and moving on.

We strongly recommend that teachers should follow up the work covered in this chapter with reference to pupils' own work. As well as private discussion with individual pupils of their personal writing, it may be helpful to organise some group discussion of specific pieces of writing. Each member of the group should be provided with a copy of the piece of work under discussion (if a pupil's work is to be discussed, it may be preferable to preserve the anonymity of the author), and asked to provide a suitable expansion: the group can then discuss which are the most successful methods of making the passage explicit.

If word-processing facilities exist in the school, a word-processor monitor is the ideal medium of presentation, as changes and corrections can be made immediately on the screen.

Answers to Exercises *pages 46–47 pupil's book*

More Differences Between Speech and Writing

A When people talk to each other, they are usually in the same place. They share the same *background* information. They can use their hands to *point* and make *gestures* to help explain what they mean. Often they use short ways of saying things, like using *pronouns* instead of *nouns*.

B 1) Go and wash your face — *it*'s filthy!
    it = face
2) Put the pens in the box where *they* usually go.
    they = pens
3) Robert put *his* coat on the peg.
    his = Robert's
4) The bandits did not know who had betrayed *them* to the police.
    them = the bandits.
5) Andy and Mike went to visit *their* gran.
    their = Andy and Mike's

BOOK THREE

  6) The tree had ivy growing all over *it*.
     it = the tree.

  7) Snow had fallen on the garden until *it* was completely covered.
     it = the garden.

C Clear instructions for the use of the machine in the picture story on page 43.

D A clear rewrite of one of the short passages on page 45.

E A clear explanation of how to play a favourite playground game.

> **Vocabulary**
> *Revises:* spoken and written language, pronoun, noun.

CHAPTER 8
Paragraphs: Chunks of Information

We introduce paragraphs here from a linguistic viewpoint — as another means of "chunking" information to aid the presentation of meaning. We are concerned first to ensure that pupils know what is meant by the term "paragraph" in a physical sense (new line, indentation of text), and then to explain that writers should organise their paragraphs to guide readers towards a clearer understanding of the message they contain. In making this latter point we touch on a number of other areas — composition, precis, higher order reading skills — which are not really within the province of this book, and which we obviously cannot cover adequately in the space available. Various other textbooks exist which cover them in detail. [For example: *What's The Idea*, *Directions*, Oliver & Boyd.]

  Two passages are given for the pupils' consideration. In each case we ask them to find the "main idea or topic" of each paragraph. This can be difficult for young readers, and patience is required. The teacher may find it helps to ask, "Can you express the main message of that paragraph in just one sentence?"

  As usual, the opportunity for pupils to reflect upon and discuss the language points arising from the chapter is more important than the eliciting of "correct" answers — although, obviously the teacher will wish to ensure that discussion is not misleading, and that acceptable answers are always provided before moving on. And, again as usual, discussion of the paragraphing in written work produced by pupils after they have studied this chapter will be particularly useful.

Answers to Exercises *page 55 pupil's book*

Paragraphs

A Writers usually split their work up into *paragraphs*. These break *texts* into sensibly-sized *chunks*. This helps a writer *organise* information for the readers.
  You usually start a new *paragraph* at a natural break in the story or text. Each *paragraph* usually deals with one *main idea* or *topic*. To start a new paragraph you start a new *line* and go in a little way from the margin.

B Questions answered in sentences, e.g.:
1) It has seven paragraphs.
2) You know a new paragraph is beginning because the writer starts a new line and indents the first line of text.
3) "Nowadays, English is probably the most widely spoken language in the world."
4) "The people of Britain originally spoke their own language."
5) There are five sentences in the fourth paragraph.
6) There are four sentences in the last paragraph.

C Paragraphed essay: *A Day in a Teacher's Life*

> **Vocabulary**
> *Revises:* sentence.
> *Introduces:* paragraph, text, main idea or topic.

CHAPTER 9
Two-Clause Sentences

This chapter begins with revision of *subject* and *verb*, which was covered earlier in this book (Chapter 4). The revision material given allows the teacher to discuss *agreement* again if he/she thinks it is necessary with the particular class. This revision material can be extended if required.

We then move on to introduce *two-clause sentences*, where two short sentences are joined by means of a conjunction (called here a "joining word"). The chapter is a fairly brief one, and the language concepts covered should be easily acquired by children of 9+. The areas of discussion about written English which are opened up by this chapter are, however, very wide-ranging. We hope that, once pupils are equipped with the necessary concepts and vocabulary, teachers will find it easier to help them improve their written work in various ways.

Perhaps the most important point to be considered with most young writers is the need for a conjunction if two clauses are to be joined together, e.g.:
   "The pirate took out his sword he thrust it at the boy."
Such constructions occur frequently in children's writing, and can be corrected either by punctuation into sentences:
   "The pirate took out his sword. He thrust it at the boy."
or by linking by means of a conjunction:
   "The pirate took out his sword and (he) thrust it at the boy."
The point to make is that *a new subject and verb have been introduced*, and that this signifies either a new clause or a new sentence.

Another area of discussion is the overuse of the conjunction "and" in some pupils' writing, where ideas are strung loosely together as in speech: "...... and ...... and ......, and, etc." It can be helpful to provide an example of such writing and discuss with a small group of children how it might be improved, either by punctuation into sentences or by the substitution of other "joining words".

With more able pupils, discussion may centre on more sophisticated stylistic conventions — the effects of varying sentence lengths, for example, or the choice

BOOK THREE

of conjunctions. The vocabulary and awareness of sentence structure acquired through study of the chapter should be of assistance in this type of discussion too. The next chapter encourages further insights into language use which can help the development of writing style.

It must be stressed again that children's writing skills will not be developed merely by studying *Mind Your Language* or any other "grammar book". Our aim is to alert pupils to the structures and conventions of written English, so that they have the concepts and vocabulary to discuss and acquire insights into written English.

> *NB.* The reason for using the term "joining word" instead of "conjunction", is that some clauses are joined by means of relative pronouns — "joining word" can be used to stand for both parts of speech. We were also wary of introducing two technical terms, "clause" and "conjunction", both with the same initial letter, in the same chapter.

Answers to Exercises *pages 60–61 pupil's book*

Sentences and Clauses

A Every sentence has at least one *subject* and one *verb*. But some sentences are made up of a number of *clauses*. Each *clause* has its own *subject* and *verb*. The *clauses* are joined together by joining words.

B
1) Dogs (S) eat (V) bones.
2) Humpty Dumpty (S) sat (V) on a wall.
3) I (S) watched (V) the boxing on TV.
4) Yesterday, my friend (S) kicked (V) me.

C
1) The weather (S) turned (V) nasty so we (S) rushed (V) indoors.
2) The Cornish (S) live (V) in Cornwall and the Welsh (S) live (V) in Wales.
3) The sweets (S) tasted (V) funny so we (S) threw (V) them away.
4) My brother (S) loves (V) swimming but I (S) hate (V) it.
5) The clock (S) struck (V) four and the children (S) dashed (V) home.

D Acceptable two-clause sentences joined with "so", "but" or "because", as in these models:

1) | I (S) was (V) angry | because my friend (S) was (V) late. |

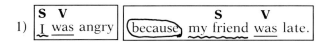

48

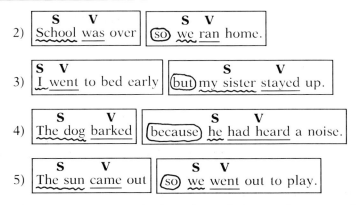

E Above sentences marked to show clauses, subjects, verbs and joining words, as shown.

> **Vocabulary**
> *Revises:* sentence, subject, verb.
> *Introduces:* clause, joining word.

CHAPTER 10
Find the Main Clause

This chapter continues the theme of sentence structure introduced in Chapter 9. The concept of two-clause sentences is briefly revised and the idea of a *main clause* is introduced. We do not define the term "main clause": as with other language concepts we merely identify all the main clauses (by underlining them), and leave it to the pupils to recognise their common elements. At the end of the chapter we ask, "In a sentence with more than one clause, how would you know which was the main clause?" Teachers should allow their pupils to study the examples and work out an answer to this question for themselves. We would hope that, guided by earlier discussion questions, they would eventually conclude that the main clause is the one which does *not* begin with a "joining word".

An important part of the chapter is the work on reorganising sentences — placing a subordinate clause *before* the main clause rather than *after* it. (Children will be familiar with opening clauses beginning with "When...", but less so with opening clauses beginning with other conjunctions such as "Because...", which are frequent in written English but rare in speech.) A conscious understanding that sentences can be reorganised in this way, without interfering with the meaning, is important to linguistic awareness. It can also contribute significantly to writing style, if the teacher encourages individual pupils to look at their own sentence-structures and aim for a variety of constructions.

In the activity "Add A Clause", pupils are requested to extend sentences by adding further clauses to some given main clauses. They should be encouraged to supply as many alternative clauses as possible to add to each main clause, and the teacher should suggest trying each clause *before* as well as *after* the main clause. Sometimes this will not be linguistically possible, but it is important that pupils notice those occasions when reorganisation will not work, as well as those when it will.

Answers to Exercises *pages 66–67 pupil's book*

Main Clauses

A   A sentence can be made up of one or more *clauses*. A one-*clause* sentence just has a *main clause*. Some sentences have a main clause and one or more other *clauses*. The main *clause* can come at the beginning, in the middle or at the end of a sentence. The *main clause* is the only clause that does not begin with a *joining word*.

B   Completed sentences (main clause added) beginning thus:
1) When Sleeping Beauty pricked her finger..........
2) If you go down to the woods today..........
3) Although it was raining..........
4) Whenever the bell rings..........
5) ....because my mum won't let me.
6) ....and I go to bed.

C   Sentences completed satisfactorily from these main clauses:
1) I put on my coat..........
2) Goldilocks did not eat the porridge..........
3) Dad painted the house..........
4) ....Superman flew away.
5) ....the dog barked.

D   Ten "joining words", e.g.
and, but, because, when, after, before, so, although, if, whenever, as, since.

E   Five two-clause sentences, using five of the conjunctions above. The same sentences, with clauses reversed, or a note "Cannot be changed", if this is the case.

> **Vocabulary**
> *Revises:* sentence, clause, subject, verb, joining word.
> *Introduces:* main clause.

CHAPTER 11
Direct Speech

Children tend to use direct speech in their written work from a very early stage: it is often difficult to follow because different speakers are not delineated in any way, and their speeches run into each other like writing of the "stream of consciousness" school. Perhaps the best way to tackle this problem is to suggest, *as soon as the child is ready*, that he/she gives each new speaker a new line, ignoring other punctuation conventions of direct speech. Inverted commas, etc., can be introduced later, perhaps after studying this chapter. What is important in the early stages is that the child becomes aware of the need to make his/her writing intentions clear, and adopts a convention which, while simple, prepares him/her for the introduction of the accepted convention later.

We point out two conventions in this chapter: first, that each new speaker is given a new paragraph; second, that inverted commas are placed around the words actually spoken. We do not mention any further complications of punctuation (e.g. commas, etc., after the spoken words and before the close of inverted commas) — these are covered in Book Four. However, those children who understand and apply the basic rules given here may benefit from having further refinements pointed out to them individually.

The work and discussion points included in the chapter are fairly straightforward. At the end, however, we suggest that a useful activity is the making up of conversations on tape, and the transcribing of these as examples of prose containing direct speech. We do not set this out as an activity, because of the difference in access to recording equipment in different classrooms — some teachers might find such an activity very difficult to organise. However, if at all possible, we recommend that as many children as possible should attempt such work. The opportunity to record their own spoken language, and to transcribe this into written language using punctuation and layout to clarify meaning, is invaluable.

Answers to Exercises *page 72 pupil's book*

Direct Speech

A When actual spoken words are used as part of a piece of writing it is called *direct speech*. We show that words are *direct speech* by enclosing them in *inverted commas*. Each new speaker gets a new *paragraph*. This helps make it clear who is speaking at any time.

B "What's for tea?" said Sally.
"Fish and chips," said Sally's mum.
"Goody!" cried Sally. "Anything else?"
"Yes. Jelly and cream," answered her mum. "Now, go and wash your hands."

C Count Dracula and Frankenstein's Monster crept through the old house.
  "Ooooh!" said a voice.
  "Who's that?" asked Dracula, but nobody replied.
  "I'm scared," said the Monster. "I want to go home."
  "Don't be silly," replied Dracula. "There's nobody here."
  "Ooooh!" said the voice again.
  "It's a ghost," wailed the Monster. "I want my mummy!"
  "I AM your mummy!" said the voice, and a figure wrapped in bandages rose up before them.
  "Argh!" screamed Dracula and the Monster together.

D Continuation of the above story, using more direct speech, correctly punctuated.

Vocabulary
Revises: comma, punctuation, paragraph.
Introduces: direct speech, inverted commas.

BOOK FOUR

CHAPTER 1
Parts of Speech

This chapter revises *nouns, verbs, pronouns, adjectives* and *adverbs*. Teachers may wish to refer to previous chapters on the particular parts of speech:

Book One	Chapter 3,4	*nouns*
Book One	Chapter 6,7	*verbs*
Book One	Chapter 9	*adjectives*
Book Two	Chapter 2	*nouns*
Book Two	Chapter 3	*verbs*
Book Two	Chapter 4	*adjectives*
Book Two	Chapter 5	*pronouns*
Book Three	Chapter 1	*nouns/verbs/adjectives*
Book Three	Chapter 2	*verbs*
Book Three	Chapter 3	*nouns/pronouns*
Book Three	Chapter 5	*adverbs*

The chapter opens with three "silly poems", each of which is used as a vehicle for revision of a particular part of speech: *verbs, nouns,* and *pronouns*. The teacher may find it necessary to supplement these activities with further work (perhaps based on activities in the chapters above) if pupils are uncertain of any of the parts of speech involved.

The "Parts of Speech Race" gives pupils an opportunity to practise recognition of nouns, verbs and pronouns in context. We recommend that pupils should be paired by the teacher for this activity: if less-able pupils are paired with able pupils they have an opportunity to learn from their peers, and the "race" is fairer.

The chapter then turns to *adjectives* and *adverbs*. Again, teachers may wish to provide some additional revision activities based on the content of previous chapters listed above.

We reintroduce here the techniques of reduction and expansion of sentences, which have been used in previous books. This illustrates how adverbs and adjectives can be used to give more descriptive detail, and to add meaning and interest to sentences. (Teachers should, of course, press home this point when discussing pupils' personal writing.) The use of reduction and expansion can also help pupils to a clearer understanding of sentence structure — letting them see the underlying framework of a sentence, and how meaning is built up on this framework. The more they are encouraged to "manipulate" language in this way, and the more confident they become in doing so, the more their use of language should benefit. Once the techniques are understood, pupils can be encouraged to look at the sentences they write themselves, to reduce them to find the basic sentence structure, and to expand them to improve their content.

Further work on reduction and expansion can be found in Chapters 4, 7, 8 and 9.

BOOK FOUR

Answers to Exercises *pages 8–9 pupil's book*

Parts of Speech

A Words have different jobs to do in a sentence. The sort of job a word does depends on what *part of speech* it is.

A noun is..........
A verb is..........
An adjective is.......... } acceptable definitions.
An adverb is..........
A pronoun..........

B Two of the following poems, with verbs, nouns, and (pronouns) marked as shown:

(Nobody) likes (me), (everybody) hates (me),

(I)'m going outside to eat worms —

Short fat juicy (ones), long thin squooshy (ones),

See how (they) squiggle and squirm!

Chop off the heads and suck out the juice

And throw (their) skins away

(Nobody) knows how much (I) thrive

On worms three times a day.

(Nobody, everybody, ones — have been used pronominally here, although only very exceptional children will recognise this!)

Little Miss Muffet
Sat on a tuffet,
Eating an Irish stew.
There came a big spider
(Who) sat down beside (her)
So Little Miss M ate (him) too.

(I) eat (my) peas with honey
(I)'ve done (it) all (my) life.
(It) makes the peas taste funny,
But (it) keeps (them) on (my) knife.

C There was an |old| man of Darjeeling

(He) travelled from London to Ealing.

(It) said on the door

"Please don't spit on the floor",

So (he) carefully spat on the ceiling.

5 verbs   7 nouns   3 pronouns   1 |adjective| 1 adverb

D 1) The girl climbed the hill.
2) A man strode into the room.
3) A horse jumps.
4) Scientists work in laboratories.
5) The wolf jumped at the girl.

E 1) Own sentence, with plenty of adjectives and adverbs. It should be accompanied by a reduced version, written and signed by a friend.
2) Own "reduced" sentence, with no adjectives or adverbs. It should be accompanied by an expanded version, written and signed by a friend.

> **Vocabulary**
> *Revises:* noun, verb, pronoun, adjective, adverb of manner, adverb of time, part of speech, sentence, reduction, expansion.

CHAPTER 2
Punctuation

Aspects of punctuation have been covered in previous books as follows:

Book One	Chapter 3	*capital/full stop*
Book One	Chapter 5	*question mark*
Book One	Chapter 8	*capital/full stop/question mark/exclamation mark*
Book Two	Chapter 7	*capital/full stop*
Book Two	Chapter 8	*full stop/question mark/exclamation mark/comma*
Book Two	Chapter 10	*apostrophe in contractions*
Book Three	Chapter 6	*full stop/question mark/exclamation mark/comma*
Book Three	Chapter 8	*paragraphing*
Book Three	Chapter 11	*inverted commas*

This chapter begins with revision of sentence punctuation (*capital letter, full stop, comma*, with brief reference to *question mark* and *exclamation mark*). Where necessary, teachers may wish to refer back to previous chapters for ideas for further revision of particular areas.

By 10 +, some children are already very proficient in the use of punctuation marks, particularly if they have come to see them as aids to conveying their meaning in writing, rather than as obscure conventions with numerous applications which have to be learnt by rote. Other pupils may, however, still be struggling to get their full stops in the right places. We hope that the revision activities offered here will have something of relevance for pupils at each of these extremes.

The chapter next moves on to discussion of brackets and dashes, of which children at this stage will be becoming increasingly aware, and which may by now be creeping into their written work. The chapter attempts to explain the rather subtle differences between these punctuation marks, and also to point out that punctuation within a sentence is very much a matter of personal choice, depending upon the author's intended meaning.

The marking of the "Punctuation Test Match" should reflect this last point: as long as the punctuation chosen for a passage divides it into acceptable sentences and helps to make its meaning clear, it can be marked correct. The teacher should deduct marks for inadequate sentence construction and for ambiguity or lack of clarity caused by punctuation (or lack of it). Each team could start with a total of, say, one hundred, and one mark be deducted for each omission or unacceptable use of punctuation marks. The team which loses the least marks is the winner.

It could then be very interesting for pupils to compare their own punctuation with that of the original versions of the passages chosen. This should provide a clear illustration that there is no one "right" or "wrong" way to punctuate a particular passage.

Answers to Exercises *pages 16–17 pupil's book*

Punctuation

A Punctuation can show the *tone* of voice in which words would be spoken. A *question mark* shows a *question*. An *exclamation mark* shows a raised voice, or that the words are not to be taken seriously.

Punctuation also shows how words should be grouped to make sense — *full stops* show the ends of sentences, *commas* show smaller breaks within sentences.

Brackets show that words are in parenthesis (aside or separate from the main sentence), and *dashes* can be used instead of brackets.

A single *dash* can show a break halfway between a *comma* and a *full stop*, but the *dash* should not be used too often.

B Passage acceptably punctuated, e.g.:
Our sun is a star. This means that it is a sphere of burning gases. The other stars we see at night are spheres of burning gases too. They look smaller than the sun because they are much, much further away. The sun is only 93 million miles away from the earth. It gives our planet the light and heat we need for life to exist here.

C Sentences acceptably punctuated, e.g.:
1) The three sections of our local library are fiction, non-fiction and reference.
2) Reference books must never be taken out of the library, but fiction and non-fiction books can be borrowed and taken home.
3) Non-fiction, which means fact, is arranged in subject groups such as history, geography, science and hobbies.
4) Fiction books are story books and are arranged on the shelves in alphabetical order of authors' names, starting at A and going on to Z.

D Sentences acceptably punctuated with commas, full stops and brackets (not dashes), e.g.:
1) A sandwich (two pieces of bread with a filling inside) takes its name from the Earl of Sandwich, who needed a convenient snack to take with him to race meetings.
2) Sir Robert Peel began the police force in the early nineteenth century, and policemen are sometimes called bobbies, because Bob is a short form of Robert.

BOOK FOUR

      3) The Earl of Cardigan gave another word to our language. He used to wear knitted woollen jackets, which became known as cardigans.
      4) Lots of household items are called after their inventors, including biros, hoovers and mackintoshes.

E   1) Own sentence, involving brackets to show parenthesis.
     2) Same sentence, with dashes instead of brackets.
     3) Own sentence involving a single dash.
     4) Same sentence using full stop or comma, whichever is more appropriate.

F   Looking at and improving own punctuation in own continuous written work.

> **Vocabulary**
> *Revises:* punctuation, full stop, exclamation mark, question mark, comma, sentence, phrase.
> *Introduces:* bracket, dash, parenthesis.

CHAPTER 3
Capital Letters

This chapter revises those uses of the capital letter which we have already covered (beginning a sentence, beginning a proper noun), and provides material through which pupils can extrapolate a number of other uses of the convention.

Most of the material presented involves considerable participation by pupils, either in pairs or as a group. As has been pointed out before, the more pupils are involved in working out the applications of the conventions of written English for themselves, the better their understanding and memory of them should be. Even if a particular child does not come up with an acceptable answer, the opportunity to *think* about the question will itself have been valuable.

Answers to Exercises *pages 22–23 pupil's book*

Capital Letters

A   A *capital* letter should always be used at the *beginning* of a sentence, and for the first letter of *proper* nouns. There are many types of proper noun, including .... [five types]. Capital letters are also required for the pronoun *I*, the first letter of each line in a *poem*, some *abbreviations*, and words referring to *God* and other important figures in world religions.

B   1) The postman delivered the letters to Orchard Road.
     2) Daffodils bloom in the springtime.
     3) There is a good film showing at the Plaza Cinema on Tuesday.
     4) Hannah said that I had not read the book by Roald Dahl.
     5) Last August I went to Spain for my holiday.

C   1) Royal Air Force — RAF
     2) Her Royal Highness — HRH
     3) Prime Minister — PM

4) Marylebone Cricket Club — MCC
5) Member of Parliament — MP
6) British Broadcasting Corporation — BBC
7) On Her Majesty's Service — OHMS
8) Please Turn Over — PTO

D 1) The PM lives at No 10 Downing Street in Westminster, which is a part of London.
2) Brazil is the largest country in South America. It is even larger than the whole of the USA.
3) A man called Bram Stoker wrote *Dracula*, but *Frankenstein* was written by a woman, Mary Shelley.
4) The eldest son of the King or Queen of England is given the title of Prince of Wales.

E *Television Programmes for Tuesday 14th March*

BBC 1	ITV. London
3.55 Up Our Street	4.00 Portland Bill
4.10 Dogtanian and the Three Muskehounds	4.10 The Blunders
	4.30 Scooby Doo
4.35 Take Two	4.45 Making of the Ark
5.00 Newsround	5.15 Connections
5.05 The Flintstones	5.45 News

Vocabulary
Revises: sentence, capital letter, proper noun.
Introduces: abbreviation.

CHAPTER 4
Spoken and Written Language

In previous books we have stressed the differences between spoken and written language, and the ways in which written language compensates for the lack of "contextual" information which is usually present in spoken language situations (See notes for Book 3, Chapter 7). Here we revise:
1) the use of punctuation to indicate tone and meaning;
2) the need for greater explicitness in written language to make up for the lack of "background information".

Some illustrations of these factors are given, and pointer questions provided to stimulate discussion. Teachers are urged to develop discussion on the differences between spoken and written language as much as possible.

The chapter then moves on to look at the translation of a spoken language incident into written language. Punctuation and greater explicitness are stressed, so that an unintelligible account using spoken language patterns becomes a clear written account. Pupils are then invited to discuss the changes. Again, the benefits of discussion cannot be overemphasised.

We point out that the written version could be improved further — teachers may wish to ask some children to carry out such improvements, by expanding the passage with descriptive content.

The issues which arise from the activities and discussion material in this chapter will have many applications within the context of pupils' own written work. Occasions where greater explicitness or clarifying punctuation are required can be pointed out and discussed with individual pupils.

> **Vocabulary**
> *Revises:* spoken and written language, punctuation, pronouns, nouns, adjectives, adverbs.

CHAPTER 5
Spoken and Written Language: Standard English

Dialect
The first section of this chapter relates to regional and cultural variations in spoken English. The way in which teachers tackle this work will depend upon which part of the country they teach in. If their pupils have particular regional or cultural accents, it will be possible to draw on these for illustrations of the points made in the chapter about accent and dialect. Nowadays, it is often possible to find a number of members of one class speaking in a number of different dialects: in such a case, there is raw material for a great deal of work on the topic. The examples we offer are a poor substitute for pupils' own spoken language. (We have, however, tried to provide examples which will be familiar to most children from television programmes.)

In the past, regional and cultural accents and dialects were often frowned on as somehow "inferior" to Standard English. Recent research in sociolinguistics shows that regional and cultural variations of English are as complex and efficient as the standard form, and that Standard English is merely another dialect, neither superior nor inferior linguistically. The real difference is that Standard English (which is, broadly speaking, the dialect of middle-class South-Easterners) has been adopted historically as the conventional *written* form of the language. All English-speaking children are therefore expected to *write* English in that dialect.

If children are told in school that the way they speak is in some way "inferior" to the standard form, they can easily become alienated from the educational system. Over recent years, therefore, teachers have been advised to accept regional and cultural variations in children's accents and dialects in their spoken English work, and not to insist on so-called "correct" English. Throughout this chapter we refer to *all* dialects in the same positive way, and hope that teachers will encourage the same attitude in discussion.

It is however, acceptable to ask pupils to *write* English in a standard dialect, if the necessity for standardisation in a written language is explained to them (or, better still, if they can work out the reasons for standardisation themselves). It is fairly obvious that, without a standard form of written English, problems with spelling, and syntactical and semantic ambiguities, could arise. Standard English usage is therefore adopted by English speakers as the *conventional* form, to ensure that everyone can understand it, no matter what their own regional or cultural variations.

In the written work of many children, therefore, many so-called "grammatical errors" are merely dialect variations — the child is writing down English as it is spoken in his geographical and cultural environment, rather than in the conventional form. In terms of that child's own spoken language, and his implicit understanding of English grammar, such variations are not errors at all: indeed, in the spoken form they are quite correct and acceptable. What he needs to understand is that written English differs from spoken English, and slight grammatical variations must therefore be learnt.

This chapter attempts to draw attention to some of the main differences between Standard English and a number of other dialects. If children are to become aware of the correct standard written form, they must first notice where their own spoken language differs from it. Once attention has been focused on this issue through the work in the chapter, it is hoped that pupils and teachers will return to the discussion whenever further examples of dialect variation occur.

Slang

The second part of the chapter is devoted to slang, which is not quite the same as dialect. Slang words and expressions tend to develop in the spoken language of particular groups of people, and using such slang is a way of expressing one's membership of the group. The groups are occasionally geographical, frequently social, and usually related to a particular generation. Slang therefore dates fairly quickly, as our examples point out.

Pupils need to learn that slang is *not* Standard English, and to define the parts of their own spoken language which are slang words and expressions. They must then search for alternative ways of expressing these in written English.

Answers to Exercises *page 35 pupil's book*

Standard English

A People speak in different ways in different parts of the country. They have different *accents* and *dialects*. And different age groups often have their own *slang* words and expressions. But written English should be the same everywhere so that everyone can understand it. It is known as *Standard English*.

B
1) We *were* late for school.
2) You *were* at home last night.
3) I *am* very tired.
4) He *was* full of energy.
5) I *was* not sure where you *were*.
6) She *was* told that they *were* coming today.

C
1) I did it this morning.
2) She has got no idea/She hasn't got any idea.
3) It was her dad who/that said it.
4) You don't know anything.
5) He didn't know my name.

D Three sentences in dialect + correct standard form.

> **Vocabulary**
> *Revises:* spoken and written English.
> *Introduces:* accent, dialect, slang.

CHAPTER 6
The Apostrophe to show Ownership

The apostrophe is possibly the most abused punctuation mark in the language. Children (and many adults), accustomed to seeing apostrophes preceding a final "s", spatter them liberally about their scripts, wherever an "s" occurs at the end of a word. They turn up in plurals ("potatoe's") in pronouns ("our's") and in other inappropriate places. Once children have learnt the correct use of the apostrophe, it might be helpful to enrol them in the "Correct-Use-of-The-Apostrophe Preservation Society" and ask them to spot abuses in the printed material in their environment: a class collection could be made.

The use of the apostrophe in contractions was covered in Book Two. We provide brief revision here — teachers may wish to supplement this with further practice before proceeding with the chapter.

The first point to be covered in our teaching of *the apostrophe to show ownership* is the concept of ownership. Children use ownership constructions in spoken language with facility, but their understanding is implicit, and needs to be made explicit before the conventions of punctuation can be explained. An "owner" is a *noun* and so is the item owned — confusion can therefore arise as to which noun is given the apostrophe (particularly if the item owned ends in a final "s"). We provide the alternative "belonging to" construction as a means of checking owner and item owned: learning to use the construction gives children an opportunity to manipulate the language involved and, through this, to become more aware of the concept of ownership.

All the examples given here are of owner-nouns ending in apostrophe + s. We do not introduce the variation (final s + apostrophe) in the chapter, as it would be extremely confusing for the majority of children. For the purposes of most children at this stage, an "apostrophe + s rule" will probably be sufficient. However, we have included the rules for the variation at the end of the chapter in a box headed "If you've managed all that, read on..." The teacher may wish particular children to look at this, or may wish to use it for a further lesson at a later date.

Once pupils have looked at the "apostrophe + s" rule to show possession, we invite them to look at some of the misuses of the apostrophe. Teachers may wish to save this section until pupils have had time to internalise the rule and are fairly confident in its use.

Answers to Exercises *pages 40–41 pupil's book*

Apostrophes to show Ownership

A An *apostrophe* is a punctuation mark that looks like a flying *comma*. It has two main uses:
    1) in *short/shortened* forms of words it shows where letters have been *missed out*;
    2) it can show *owner*ship. Where a noun is an "owner", you add an *apostrophe + s*, to show *owner*ship.

B 1) Matthew's coat — the coat belonging to Matthew
    2) Alexander's drum — the drum belonging to Alexander
    3) Mum's cup — the cup belonging to Mum

4) The postman's bag — the bag belonging to the postman
5) Andy's book — the book belonging to Andy
6) Hannah's hair — the hair belonging to Hannah
7) The teacher's name — the name belonging to the teacher

C 1) The knight's armour was very heavy.
2) We made our way up to Count Dracula's castle.
3) The lion's mane was thick and matted.
4) Dick Turpin's horse was called Black Bess.
5) I picked up the children's books.
6) Monday's child is fair of face,
7) Tuesday's child is full of grace.

D At least four examples of apostrophe to show ownership taken from books. "Belonging to" version written beside each one.

E Many writers have used pen names to conceal their identity. Samuel Clemens, for instance, wrote books under the name of Mark Twain. Twain's books included *Tom Sawyer* and *Huckleberry Finn*. Lewis Carroll's real name was Charles Dodgson — he was a University lecturer who disguised himself to write *Alice's Adventures in Wonderland*. And perhaps the most famous of all children's writers also had a pen-name — Enid Blyton's real name was Darryl Waters.

> **Vocabulary**
> *Revises:* noun, pronoun, verb, adjective, plural, apostrophe in contractions.
> *Introduces:* apostrophe to show ownership.

CHAPTER 7
Expanding and Reducing Sentences (Subjects, Verbs and Clauses)

This chapter revises two areas of sentence structure:
1) subjects and verbs (covered in Book Two, Chapters 3, 4, and 5, and Book Three, Chapters 1, 2 and 4);
2) Two-clause sentences (covered in Book Three, Chapters 9 and 10).

Teachers may wish to refer back to these chapters and provide some revision material based on them before proceeding.

We concentrate here on the important linguistic procedures of expansion and reduction. If a reader can identify the basic structural elements of a sentence (subject and verb of each clause), he will be better able to read difficult material with understanding, and to monitor his own sentence construction in writing. The best way to carry out such identification is to find the verb and to *reduce* the subject to a simple pronoun. The converse of reduction is, of course, *expansion*, and practice in expanding subjects can be helpful in encouraging more explicitness in writing.

We first give examples of and practice in expansion and reduction of the subject in a simple, one-clause sentence. The chapter then proceeds to look at two-clause sentences, where the subject of each clause can be expanded or reduced.

Finally, we look at a few three-clause sentences, and the effects of expansion and reduction here.

This chapter illustrates the need for early learning of the names of parts of speech and other linguistic terms. If pupils are possessed of a metalanguage with which to discuss such activities as the ones suggested in this chapter, they will be at a considerable advantage in the use of language generally.

Answers to Exercises *pages 47–48 pupil's book*

Expanding and Reducing Sentences

A Every sentence has a *subject* and a *verb*. Sentences with more than one clause have a *subject* and a *verb* in each *clause*. The subjects can be long or just one word (such as a *pronoun*).

B
1) The baby [S] cried [V] loudly.
2) A large green monster [S] crawled [V] out of the swamp.
3) It [S] is [V] cloudy.
4) Mr and Mrs Jones [S] went [V] home.
5) Earlier, Mr and Mrs Jones [S] went [V] home.

C Subjects expanded in the following sentences:
1) He danced.
2) She smiled.
3) We were tired.
4) It was wonderful.
5) They fell asleep.

D
1) It neighed softly.
2) They came out of the woods.
3) They were all runners.

E All subjects expanded in the following sentences:
1) She waved and he blushed.
2) Until he arrived, she was the tallest.
3) After it had eaten, they took it into the garden.
4) When he went to sleep, she exchanged his tooth for ten pence.

F
1) They charged and they ran away.
2) When they went to bed she collapsed, exhausted.
3) They came to tea but it had all been eaten.

> **Vocabulary**
> *Revises:* subject, verb, clauses, main clause, pronoun, joining word, expansion, reduction.

BOOK FOUR

CHAPTER 8
Subjects, Verbs and Objects

The chapter begins with a brief reference to subject and verb, which were covered at length in the last chapter. Unless a great deal of time has elapsed since the last chapter was covered, there should be no necessity for further revision.

The *object* of a sentence is introduced through examples, and pupils are then asked to identify the objects in a number of sentences. If pupils experience difficulties, it may be helpful to try the following exercise:

Divide a piece of paper into three:
Label the sections as shown.
Fill in a number of short
sentences, as our examples.
Discuss which are S, V and O.

Who? What?	Did What?	To Whom To What
The cat	tangled	the wool
I	ate	an ice cream

Some *reduction* and *expansion* exercises follow. The teacher may wish to give further examples of the same type, if necessary.

We introduce the term "transitive verb" as part of our explanation of SVO sentences, merely for our own convenience in subsequent explanations. It is not at all necessary for pupils to remember this term, or to use it themselves unless they wish to do so.

We also introduce the term "adverbial" in the explanation of the SILLY GOSSIP game — we had to call the "adverbial" section something, so we called it by its correct linguistic label. Again, however, pupils need not memorise or utilise this term themselves.

Once the rules have been established, SILLY GOSSIP has proved to be a popular game with classes, and they may wish to play it repeatedly, when spare time is available. The more often they *do* play it, the more likely it is that the vocabulary and concepts concerned will be learned.

We do not introduce multi-clause SVO sentences (e.g. SVO + SVO) because of shortage of space. Teachers may, however, wish to discuss such structures with their pupils.

Answers to Exercises *pages 53–54 pupil's book*

Subjects, Verbs and Objects

A Every sentence has a *subject* and a *verb*. Some sentences also have an *object*. The *object* can be a person or a thing, which usually has something done to it in the sentence. Not all *verbs* take *objects*. *Objects*, like *subjects*, can be expanded or reduced.

B 1) The gardener (S) pruned (V) the roses (O).

2) Mrs. Beeton (S) wrote (V) a cookery book (O).

3) In Wonderland, Alice (S) met (V) a white rabbit (O).

BOOK FOUR

                     S   V   O
4) To stop the match, the referee blew his whistle.

       S   V   O
5) Damian threw the ball over the wall.

C Objects expanded in these sentences:
   1) The policeman caught him.
   2) I hate it.
   3) Children like them.
   4) The army attacked it.
   5) The teacher praised her.

D 1) They wore them.
   2) She knighted him on board his ship.
   3) Later, he defeated it.
   4) He produced them.
   5) I (or he/she is) am wearing shoes.

E Three short SVO sentences, labelled SVO.

> **Vocabulary**
> *Revises:* subject, verb, expansion, reduction.
> *Introduces:* object, (transitive verb, adverbial).

CHAPTER 9
Inverted Commas

The use of inverted commas to signal direct speech was introduced in Book Three, Chapter 11. Here we begin with a brief discussion of other occasions on which inverted commas can be employed. Pupils are invited to extrapolate from examples that inverted commas can be used for signalling titles (of e.g. books, poems, programmes, songs, etc.) and to indicate that a word is being treated as an object of discussion, rather than used for its sense.

   We also ask pupils to look out for other occasions on which inverted commas are employed. They may notice them being used to signal words or expressions which are employed in an unusual way, or in an unusual context. Writers quite often "point" to words in this way, to show that they are "a teeny bit inappropriate". The authors suggest that teachers urge pupils not to adopt this rather "lazy-looking" technique too frequently.

   In Book Three we gave two rules only for the treatment of direct speech:
1) Start each new speaker on a new line (new paragraph);
2) Put inverted commas round the words actually spoken.

   If pupils have internalised these rules, they should be able to learn the remaining rules of punctuation of direct speech with little difficulty. The activity with the passage from Richmal Crompton's "William" story requires that they look carefully at these punctuation conventions, and work out the remaining rules for themselves. Briefly, these rules are:
1) punctuation of the spoken words is according to normal conventions and is

placed inside the inverted commas;
2) spoken words are separated from a subsequent dialogue-carrier (e.g. "said David") by a comma inside the inverted commas, unless they require a question mark or exclamation mark at that point, in which case this is placed within the inverted commas;
3) a preceding dialogue-carrier is separated from the direct speech by a comma before the inverted commas;
4) the words in inverted commas always begin with a capital letter, unless the dialogue-carrier has interrupted a sentence mid-way, in which case the second part of the direct speech may begin with a small-case letter;

After the rules have been discussed, there is a short passage of direct speech which is to be written on the blackboard and punctuated by the class as a whole. Further discussion may arise as a result of this activity.

Answers to Exercises *pages 59–60 pupil's book*

Inverted Commas

A *Inverted commas* are used to show *direct* speech. They are placed around the words actually spoken. Any punctuation which goes with the *direct* speech is included *inside* the *inverted commas*. A *comma* is usually used to separate the direct speech from the rest of the sentence (unless a *question mark* or *exclamation mark* is required).

Inverted commas can also be used around the titles of books, films, etc., and around words which are being discussed in a piece of writing.

B 1) Betsy Byars is an American authoress whose books include "The Eighteenth Emergency" and "The Midnight Fox".
2) The Walt Disney film "One Hundred and One Dalmatians" has a villainess called Cruella de Ville.
3) Bob Geldof wrote a song called "Do They Know It's Christmas?" to help the starving people of Africa.
4) My mum and dad argue because she wants to watch "Sports Grandstand" and he wants to watch the film on the other channel.

C A passage of direct speech from a novel, about half a page long, blocked in colour as in the *William* extract. Punctuation should be clearly shown.

D Short story taken from a cartoon strip. The narrative may vary from this example, but direct speech (especially punctuation) should be similar:

Biffo and Buster were out one snowy day.
"Let's go and build a snowman on the common," said Biffo.
They made a big snowman and then Biffo took some things out a sack.
"There!" he said, "And I've got just the stuff to finish him off, Buster!"
They put a tin hat on the snowman, a carrot for a nose, some coal for eyes and teeth and a stick for a walking stick.
Then Biffo began to feel the cold.
"Chilly, isn't it?" he said. "Let's have some soup!"
"B-but how?" asked Buster.
"Just watch!" said Biffo, taking the things from the snowman. He made a fire

with the coal, used the tin hat for a pot, made carrot soup with the carrot and some snow, and stirred it with the stick!

"Carrot soup coming up!" said Biffo.

"Great!" said Buster. "Slurp!"

> **Vocabulary**
> *Revises:* inverted commas, direct speech, other punctuation marks.

CHAPTER 10
Words and Meanings: Idioms

The English language abounds in idioms, which fluent speakers of the language use without considering their literal meaning or the ambiguities of meaning their use can create. Our lack of awareness of idioms indicates the extent to which our use of language is implicitly, rather than explicitly, understood. Non-English speakers are often bemused by the wide array of apparent nonsense we speak!

Children are usually slightly more aware of idioms than adults, because they are continually meeting ones which are new to them, and having to sort out their meaning. They will therefore probably recognise that sorting out what one *can* and *cannot* say in English can be a problem.

Research in America has shown that at 10+ children should be capable of explaining why constructions of the type given in the first four examples are not acceptable in English. Such an activity requires them to look at language objectively — at its semantic rather than its syntactic side. Discussion here should be valuable.

The following work, on idioms themselves, should be self-explanatory, and the activity IDIOTIC IDIOMS gives an opportunity for children to exercise their semantic ingenuity.

The chapter concludes with a brief glance at the different words and idioms of another country: Americanisms.

> **Vocabulary**
> *Introduces:* idiom

CHAPTER 11
Sorts of Sentences and Sentence Transformations

In this chapter we look at the ways in which a basic sentence can be *transformed* by a proficient speaker of the language. We introduce the terms *statement (positive* and *negative), question* and *command* to define the basic types of sentence, and invite children to identify examples of each and then to change simple sentences from one type to another.

The amount of new vocabulary introduced in the chapter is greater than usual. However, to children of 11+ most of the new words listed above should be familiar from other contexts — in discussion, teachers could draw on children's knowledge of these words as used in the following examples:

He made a **statement** to the police.
We received a bank **statement** through the post.
I'm **positive** that's the right way.
The results of the tests for rabies were **positive**.
"Have you identified the alien spaceship, captain?"
   "**Negative**."
The envelope contained photographic **negatives**.

In the section on *commands*, we introduce yet another term: *understood*. Again, this word will be familiar from other contexts and should thus be fairly memorable.

We have been generally reluctant to overload pupils with new vocabulary in this way throughout the series, but it has been unavoidable in this case, due to lack of space. We do therefore urge teachers to give plenty of opportunity in discussion for practice of the words' new meanings, and to check when possible that pupils have internalised them correctly.

The activity, "Using the Rules: Sentence Transformation", pulls together much of what the pupils have learnt throughout the series about the way language works. It employs many of the technical linguistic terms ("metalanguage") that they have learnt in order to talk about language. It also demonstrates a great deal about how English works as a language system — we believe that a child who is able to complete this activity satisfactorily (and, even better, to exercise the transformations on his own self-generated SVO sentence) has achieved a creditable degree of linguistic awareness.

We recommend that, for the activity "Messing About With A Sentence", poorer pupils should be teamed with more able pupils, so that they may pick up ideas and perhaps achieve more understanding from assisting their more confident peers.

Answers to Exercises *page 69 pupil's book*

Sentences

A We can describe *sentences* in terms of the jobs they do. A sentence that tells you something is called a *statement*. It can be *positive* or *negative*. A sentence can also be a *question* or a *command* (in *commands* the subject is *understood*).

B 1) a) command,   b) negative.
    2) a) statement, b) positive.
    3) a) question,   b) positive.
    4) a) question,   b) negative.
    5) a) command,   b) positive.
    6) a) command,   b) negative.
    7) a) statement, b) positive.
    8) a) question,   b) negative.
    9) a) question,   b) negative.
   10) a) command,   b) positive.

C Statements changed into acceptable questions, e.g.:
1) Is Jamie older than you?
2) Is he really frightened?
3) Do tadpoles turn into frogs?
4) Did the Great Fire of London start in Pudding Lane?
5) Can transitive verbs take an object?

D Short SVO sentence transformed in seven ways:
1) changed to negative,
2) changed to question,
3) change of tense,
4) changed to plural/singular,
5) expanded with additional words,
6) reduced by changing nouns to pronouns,
7) expanded by additional clause.

> **Vocabulary**
> *Introduces:* statement, positive, negative, command, understood, transform.
> *Revises:* noun, verb, adjective, adverb, pronoun, sentence, question, tense, singular, plural, subject, object, clause, punctuation.

CHAPTER 12
What is Language?

In this final chapter we ask children to consider the characteristics of language. The chapter consists entirely of discussion material (including a piece of narrative for discussion, on the subject of a "talking ape" in the USA).

The discussion material is all open-ended — academics are not in agreement on "right" or "wrong" answers in this area, so it does not matter if agreement cannot be reached in the classroom! It is the opportunity to talk about the topic which is important, along with the possibility that pupils will be alerted to questions of language, which they may continue to consider for themselves.

Teachers may find it useful to know that most psycholinguists would include a selection of the following points in their definitions of the nature of human language:

1) it is produced and received through the vocal-auditory channels;
2) the symbols (words) used are arbitrary — there is no reason why "dog" should be the word for a dog;
3) words have semanticity (meanings which are appreciated by all users of that language) — the symbols therefore come to represent the objects or actions to which they refer;
4) the language is handed down from one generation to another;
5) human speech is spontaneous — we can speak without the need for a particular stimulus (whereas animals often "speak" only in response to a particular situation);
6) human beings generally take it in turns to speak — human conversation is

thus unlike animal communication;
7) the basic units of articulation (sounds like "P", "I" and "N") are meaningless in themselves, but can be combined into various meaningful sequences (e.g. PIN and NIP);
8) language can be used to refer to things which are distant in place and time (thus allowing a very wide range of thought and discussion);
9) human language is structure-dependent — that is, the order of words is of great significance. Human beings can automatically reorganise chunks of language by strict rules to convey their meaning;
10) it is creative — human beings can talk about anything they like, however silly, without any difficulties linguistically (I can, if I wish, speculate about a "three-legged kangaroo wearing a pink beret").

It is hoped that pupils' discussions of the properties of language will create some areas of dispute and contention in the classroom, and that the (reasoned) argument that ensues may touch on the essence of some of these points.

SELECTED BIBLIOGRAPHY

Teachers wishing to read further in the subject of language and language awareness may find these titles provide a useful introduction to the subject.

Aitchison, J. (1984) *The Articulate Mammal*, Hutchinson University Library.

Crystal, D. (1976) *Child Language, Learning and Linguistics: an overview for the teaching and therapeutic professions*, Edward Arnold.

Downing, J. (1979) *Reading and Reasoning*, Chambers.

Donaldson, M. (1984) *Children's Minds*, Fontana.

Ferreiro, E. and Teberosky, A. (1983) *Literacy Before Schooling*, Heinemann Educational Books.

Francis, H. (1982) *Learning To Read*, Unwin Educational Books.

Kingman, Sir J et al (1988) *Report of the Committee of Inquiry into the Teaching of English Language*, HMSO.

Olson, D.R. (1984) *See! Jumping! Some Oral Antecedents of Literacy*, from *Awakening to Literacy*, ed. Goelman, Oberg and Smith, University of Victoria.

Perera, K. (1984) *Children's Writing and Reading*, Blackwell.

Slobin, D.I. (1978) *Psycholinguistics*, Scott, Foresman and Co.

Smith, F. (1978) *Reading*, CUP.

Smith, F. (1982) *Writing and the Writer*, Heinemann Educational Books.

Stubbs, M. (1980) *Language and Literacy*, Routledge & Kegan Paul.

Trudgill, P. (1974) *Sociolinguistics*, Penguin.

Vygotsky, L.S. (1962) *Thought and Language*, Routledge & Kegan Paul.

Waterhouse, L., Fischer, K.M. and Ryan, E.B. (1981) *Language Awareness and Reading*, International Reading Association.